D0995029

Roadcraft

THE POLICE DRIVER'S HANDBOOK

HMSO

Author: Philip Coyne
Design and illustration: Bill Mayblin
Editor: Penny Mares
Research: Philip Coyne, Bill Mayblin, Penny Mares

The authors and working group wish to acknowledge
the contribution of Dr. Robert West to the contents of
chapter 1.

Cover photographs courtesy of the Metropolitan Police

The Police Foundation

The Police Foundation is an independent research
charity working to improve the effectiveness of
policing and the relationship between police services
and the communities they serve.

National Extension College

The National Extension College is an educational trust
and a registered charity with a distinguished body of
trustees. It is an independent, self-financing
organisation. Since it was established in 1963, NEC
has pioneered the development of flexible learning for
adults. NEC is actively developing innovative materials
and systems for distance learning opportunities on
over 100 courses, from basic skills and general
education to degree and professional training.

For further details of NEC's resources and courses
contact:

Customer Services Department
National Extension College
18 Brooklands Avenue
Cambridge CB2 2HN

Tel: 01223 358295
Fax: 01223 313586

Acknowledgments

This new edition of *Roadcraft* was initiated by The Police Foundation at the request of the Association of Chief Police Officers. It was produced by the National Police Driving Schools' Conference Roadcraft Working Party in conjunction with the Police Foundation and the National Extension College.

The Police Foundation would like to thank the many individuals and organisations who gave so freely of their time and expertise in the preparation of this edition of *Roadcraft*.

This edition of *Roadcraft* has been approved by the Association of Chief Police Officers, which is satisfied that it reflects current best practice in police driving instruction and takes into account the relevant views of civilian experts.

Contents

Chapter 5
Skidding

Chapter 6
Driver's signals

Chapter 7

Positioning

Chapter 8

Cornering

Chapter 11
Speed and safety

Appendices

About *Roadcraft*

How can *Roadcraft* help your driving?

The aim of *Roadcraft* is to improve the skill and safety of your driving so that you can make the best use of road and traffic conditions. Driving safety and driving skill are aspects of the same ability – the ability to control the position and speed of your vehicle relative to everything else on the road. An accident or even a near miss usually represents a loss of this control – a lapse in driving skill. *Roadcraft* aims to help you improve your skills by increasing your awareness of the range of factors that affect your driving – your own capabilities, the characteristics of your vehicle, and the road and traffic conditions.

Roadcraft is the handbook for police drivers undertaking police driver training. In police training *Roadcraft* is combined with practical instruction. This edition is designed so that it can be used for self study either before or during a course, and for ready reference afterwards.

What vehicles does *Roadcraft* cover?

Roadcraft is written with a modern car in mind but the advice it contains is relevant to both older and larger vehicles. You do, however, need to adapt your driving to the different characteristics of these vehicles.

The basic design and the supplementary aids built into a vehicle significantly affect its handling characteristics. These vary widely between vehicles and it is not possible in a book of this size to cover every variation in wheel-drive, power ratio, traction control, adaptive suspension or antilock braking system (ABS). To drive well you need to adapt your driving to the characteristics of your vehicle, so it is important to know and follow the manufacturer's guidance.

What *Roadcraft* does not include

Roadcraft assumes that you are thoroughly familiar with the contents of the current edition of the *Highway Code* and the *Know your Traffic Signs* booklet. Advice and instructions contained in these publications are not generally repeated in *Roadcraft*.

Special techniques, such as those used in emergency response or pursuit driving, are not covered in *Roadcraft*. We recommend that drivers consult their instructors and the appropriate codes of practice for guidance in these areas. Techniques which require a high level of instructional guidance to ensure their safety have also been excluded. Your instructor will introduce you to these techniques when appropriate.

Using *Roadcraft* for self study

Roadcraft has a number of features to make it easier to use and to help you check your learning.

- At the start of each chapter there is a *Use this chapter to find out* section. This identifies the main learning points of the chapter. Use it to help you select the chapters or sections that you need to concentrate on.
- Illustrations and diagrams are used to explain complex ideas. They are an essential part of the book and often contain information not explained elsewhere.
- Key points are highlighted in yellow.
- Throughout the text you will find questions and activities. These are designed to help you check your understanding and assess your progress. Many of the activities are practical, helping you to transfer the advice in *Roadcraft* to your everyday driving.
- At the end of each chapter there is a review of the key points and questions to help you check your understanding.

We suggest that you keep a notebook for making your own notes and for completing the written activities. This will help you to organise your work and will provide a readily available record for reviewing your own progress.

Working through the chapters

Chapters 1, 2 and 3 set out the basic principles and information on which later chapters build so you should ideally read these in sequence first. If you are using *Roadcraft* as part of a driving course, consult your instructor who may want you to study certain sections of the book in a different order.

The importance of practice

Just reading *Roadcraft* will not make you a better driver. Practice is an essential part of learning any skill. What matters is not how well you can recall the content of this book but how well you can apply what you have learnt to your driving. Many of the techniques explained in *Roadcraft* are fairly simple in themselves. Finesse in driving skill comes from applying them consistently. All the techniques depend on judgement and this only comes with practice. Many of the activities designed to help you practise techniques can be carried out during your everyday driving. Your goal should be to apply the techniques in *Roadcraft* systematically so that they become an everyday part of your driving.

You cannot absorb all the information in *Roadcraft* in one reading, so we suggest that you read a section, select a technique, practise it, assess your progress, and then refer back to *Roadcraft* to refine the technique further. The text has been designed to help you do this.

Using *Roadcraft* for reference

Each chapter contains cross-references to relevant information in other chapters. The contents pages at the front of the book list all the main headings and a selective list of the most useful sub-headings. There is an index on page 175 to make it easier to find the information you want. There is also a glossary on page 172 which explains key terms.

Learning is a continuous process

Being a good driver means that you never stop learning. To improve your skills you must be prepared to take responsibility for your own learning. This means that you need to constantly review and, where necessary, adapt your driving to maintain standards and improve techniques. Vehicles and driving conditions are constantly changing, and your skills need to keep pace with this change, otherwise they will become outdated, inappropriate and dangerous. Whenever you drive, regard it as an opportunity to reassess and improve your skills. Only by constantly developing your insight and knowledge can you fulfil your responsibility to drive safely and effectively.

Becoming a better driver

The mental characteristics of a good driver

This chapter is about how you can become a better driver. It focuses not on the physical but on the mental aspects of driving skills, and looks at how attitudes and concentration affect driving performance.

Research evidence shows that attitudes affect driving safety, but developing appropriate attitudes is not simple. It depends on recognising that attitudes are important, and on making a personal commitment to change attitudes that are unsafe. The first part of the chapter looks at the pattern of traffic accidents in Great Britain, and at what the research evidence tells us about who is at greatest risk of having an accident. Understanding this evidence can be an important step in recognising and changing inappropriate attitudes.

Traffic accidents

Most drivers think they are both safer and more skilful than the average driver – but we cannot all be right. In more than 90% of traffic accidents, human error is the cause; accidents do not just happen by chance, they are the consequence of unsafe driving practices. Driving safety cannot be thought of as an add-on extra; it has to be built into the way you drive.

Road accidents

Traffic accidents account for:

almost half of all accidental deaths in Britain

nearly a quarter of all adult deaths under 30, whether accidental or not

the largest single cause of death and injury for young adults.

Your likelihood of having an accident

Average drivers cover about 10,000 miles a year and have a one in seven chance of an accident during that time. Some types of driver are more at risk than others:

- those travelling more miles than average per year
- men
- younger drivers
- inexperienced drivers.

What are the likeliest sorts of accidents?

We can also tell from the statistics which are the commonest types of accident:

- about a third of all accidents are rear end shunts – where one vehicle crashes into the back of another
- a quarter of all accidents are caused by one vehicle driving across another vehicle's priority
- around one sixth of all accidents involve a loss of directional control.

Do we learn from our mistakes?

Drivers at risk

Sadly the evidence shows that we do not learn very well from our mistakes. Even after taking account of age, sex, annual mileage and driving experience, some drivers are consistently more at risk than others:

- if you have had an accident in one three-year period you are twice as likely to have another accident in the next three years
- if you have had an accident for which you could be held at least partly responsible, you are four times more likely to have a similar accident in the next year.

Repeating accidents

Drivers also tend to repeat the types of accident they have. If you have hit another vehicle from behind you are twice as likely as the average driver to do so again. If you have crashed into another vehicle after pulling out into its path in one three-year period, you are three times more likely than normal to have a similar accident in the next three years.

Driving too close

The practice of driving too close behind the vehicle in front gives a valuable insight into the way accidents happen. Because errors go unpunished – that is, they are not always followed by an accident – they develop into bad habits which increase the risk that one day the driver will be involved in an accident. Driving too close to the vehicle in front is probably the worst of these bad practices.

Driving too close to the vehicle in front is one of the commonest causes of accidents. It is so common that most drivers see no risk in it. Half the rear end shunts occur when the vehicle in front brakes sharply and the one behind does not stop in time.

Resistance to learning from experience

These facts show that we are not very good at learning from experience. Most drivers involved in an accident do not accept that they contributed to it. If you think that you did not help to cause an accident, you will also think that you have nothing to learn from it, and your driving technique, together with any faults that contributed to the accident, will remain unchanged.

To become a better driver, we have to recognise the resistance in ourselves to accepting responsibility, and take steps to overcome it. The first step is to recognise that we all have a resistance to learning. **Once we have learnt to do something routinely we are very reluctant to alter that routine, whatever the evidence that it does not work.**

Every near miss and accident needs to be seen as an opportunity to re-evaluate and improve your driving technique.

Have you experienced a near miss or accident?

Have you been involved in a near miss or accident in the last three years?

☐ yes   ☐ no

If the answer is yes, did the incident involve:

☐ a rear end shunt?
☐ one vehicle driving across another's priority?
☐ driver losing control of the vehicle?

Did the incident involve a driver (that might include you) in one of the higher than average risk categories:

☐ a driver covering more miles than average per year?
☐ a male driver?
☐ a younger driver?
☐ an inexperienced driver?

What have you learnt from the experience?

An ability to be self-critical and learn from experience is one of the key attributes of a good driver. The next sections look at other positive and negative attitudes that influence driving skill.

What makes a good driver?

Good drivers have a quiet efficiency in their actions and this derives from:

- a good level of attention
- accurate observation
- matching the vehicle's speed and direction to the situation
- awareness of the risks inherent in particular road and traffic situations
- acting to keep identified risks to a minimum
- awareness of their own limitations and those of the vehicle and the roads
- skilful use of vehicle controls.

It is not simply the speed of your reactions that determines whether you are a safe driver but your ability to identify and respond to hazards. Being able to respond quickly to simple stimuli such as noise and light does not in itself reduce accident risks. Young, inexperienced drivers typically have very fast reactions to simple stimuli but have slow reactions to traffic hazards.

The ability to detect hazards is learnt like any other skill and depends partly on experience. More experienced drivers develop a sensitivity to the early indications of possible trouble. When risks arise they monitor them at a subconscious level in readiness to respond quickly if the situation develops dangerously. Because they are more aware of potential danger they are more alert while driving, and this helps to sustain their concentration. (For more on concentration and attention see page 7.)

How attitude affects good driving

How would you describe your attitude

to other road users?

to speed?

to risk taking?

Studies have shown that drivers' attitudes to other road users, speed and risk taking are a good guide to their likelihood of having an accident. Later in this section there is an opportunity for you to try two examples of attitude tests used in research studies.

Attitudes to other road users

Good driving depends on constructive attitudes and consideration for other road users. There is already a great deal of potential conflict on the roads without adding to it by selfish and aggressive behaviour. Such behaviour increases the stress levels of other drivers and increases the risk of accidents. Many drivers become unnecessarily angry when other road users interrupt their progress. You can reduce the risk of accidents for yourself and everyone else by being more tolerant and by avoiding actions which create unnecessary stress.

Attitudes to speed

The speed at which you drive is one of the most important factors in determining your risk of having an accident. The faster you go, the less chance you have of taking avoiding action, and the greater your risk of having an accident. Speed is largely a matter of choice – the occasions when it is absolutely necessary to drive fast are fairly limited. Good driving requires you to drive at a speed that is safe for the conditions.

Attitudes to risk taking

There is always some degree of risk associated with driving because it involves moving a large heavy object at relatively high speeds, but a driver's attitudes can greatly influence the risk involved. Attitudes which predispose you to risk are:

- enjoying the thrill of danger
- enjoying impressing passengers or other drivers
- disregarding personal safety
- the illusion of control, or overestimating your ability
- justifying risks because they are taken in a noble cause.

Young, inexperienced drivers run the greatest risk of accidents because they have a greater tendency to seek risk and disregard danger. They also see less risk in many traffic situations than more experienced drivers.

Many drivers take risks to impress other people – for example, young male drivers tend to drive faster when they have young male passengers than when alone or with female passengers.

Drivers tend to suffer from the illusion of control, which is a tendency to overestimate their ability to cope with the demands of traffic when they are driving. This undermines the accurate perception of risk.

Police drivers, like drivers in the other emergency services, need to be aware that risks cannot be justified by telling themselves that they are taking the risks in a noble cause – to help someone else, or to catch a person suspected of a crime. Your overriding responsibility in any situation is to drive safely, and that is what you should be thinking about while you are driving to an emergency. If you have an accident and you fail to arrive, you are no help to the people in need. If you injure yourself or someone else on the way you will have turned an emergency into a tragedy, and will still have done nothing to help. Your objective should be to arrive as quickly as is safely possible, and *Roadcraft* is designed to help you do that.

Red mist

'Red mist' is the term used to describe the state of mind of drivers who are so determined to achieve some objective – catching a vehicle in front, getting to an incident in the shortest possible time, overtaking another driver – that they are no longer capable of realistically assessing driving risks. Their minds are not on their driving but on some other goal; they have become emotionally and physiologically caught up in the chase. Red mist can affect all drivers, but drivers in the emergency services need to be particularly aware of the problem. This section focuses on the needs of police drivers, but other drivers may also find it helpful.

Drivers suffering from red mist tend to ignore normal risk factors such as wet roads, heavy traffic or urban conditions, and the outcome is a significant increase in accidents. It is important to recognise that this happens as much in short pursuits at relatively slow speeds as in fast motorway pursuits. It is a significant problem which drivers need to take steps to avoid.

To prevent red mist, drivers need to be able to maintain their usual calm considered approach when responding to emergencies. The key to this is to concentrate on the driving task in hand rather than on the incident. Above all, avoid thinking about what is happening at the scene of the incident, or personalising the conflict with the driver you are pursuing.

Individuals vary in the strategy they use to help them concentrate on driving in these situations. Some drivers find that deciding to think only about their driving is enough. Others remind themselves of the horrific consequences of driving dangerously, or that the incident they are responding to will have changed from the report, no matter how quickly they arrive. Each driver has to find their own method of keeping calm and concentrating, but the key steps in helping to prevent red mist are set out below.

Do not get into a personality conflict with a driver you are pursuing. Be dispassionate about the task and concentrate on behaviour rather than personality. Use deliberately neutral, non-aggressive language to describe the other driver (to yourself as well as to others).

- Do not imagine what you are likely to find at the incident – assess the incident when you arrive at it.
- Concentrate on your driving – if you find this difficult, try giving yourself a running commentary on your driving, spoken aloud.

Other causes of risk taking

Greater risk taking also arises from attitudes that have nothing directly to do with risk assessment. Impatient, aggressive and selfish attitudes can all influence the way people drive. These factors are all linked with excessive speed and a tendency to commit other driving violations that put the drivers at risk (such as driving through red lights, 'undertaking' and driving too close).

A disregard for social values (such as defrauding insurance companies, illegal parking, tax evasion, not paying TV licences and a general disregard for the law) has been specifically identified with an increased risk of accident. Rash decision making also increases the risk. If you do not consider all the implications of your decisions, your actions are unpredictable and you fail to take account of traffic conditions.

Emotional mood and accident risk

Drivers commonly express how they feel in the way that they drive, and this can be very dangerous. Drivers who have recently had an argument behave more aggressively than normal and drive too fast and too close to the vehicle in front. American research shows that there is a greater risk of an accident during times of stress such as during divorce proceedings.

Traffic delays are a common source of stress and frustration. Many drivers release this anger by driving more aggressively and by taking more risks. If you are able to recognise this as a problem and can find other ways of coping with the stress you will improve your driving. Focusing on the present rather than on the purpose of the journey is one way of reducing the stress.

Attitudes and society

Our attitudes are shaped to a large degree by the society which we live in, the organisations we belong to and the company we keep. These groups help us to define what is normal, what is acceptable and what is desirable. We take on the attitudes of those with whom we identify. This is partly because it helps us

How do mood and stress affect your driving?

Can you pinpoint things that may have affected your mood while driving during the past week, for example:

☐ a source of long-term or serious stress in your life?

☐ an argument or other incident causing you short-term stress?

☐ daily sources of frustration in the journeys you make?

How often do you get angry with other drivers?

☐ Never ☐ Rarely ☐ Sometimes ☐ Quite often ☐ Very often

How does anger affect your behaviour?

What in the past have you done to control your anger?

to feel good about ourselves and partly because we look for approval from those whose views we care about.

Large organisations can affect attitudes to road safety through educational and publicity material. They can adopt policies that reward safe driving and punish unsafe driving. This is why it is particularly important that police drivers are seen to be exemplary drivers. The attitude that police drivers take towards their driving will be noticed by society at large and will influence other drivers.

Because the attitudes of your colleagues and the organisation you work for affect your driving, you should be aware of what these attitudes are. Certain attitudes – for example, an overemphasis on reaching destinations on time, using language which is stereotyping or aggressive, or valuing speed and competitiveness – may undermine safe driving practices. Problems such as these really need to be dealt with at an organisational level, but the first step in remedying them is to acknowledge that they exist and that they have a personal relevance.

You need to be aware of the social influences on attitudes and safety but, in the end, the responsibility for the safety of yourself and other road users is yours alone. Most people are reactive; if they encounter another driver with a courteous attitude and an obvious concern for safety, they are encouraged to adopt a similar approach. Drivers who have a professional attitude to driving and safety can influence the behaviour of other motorists for the better.

Changing unhelpful attitudes

Develop positive attitudes

We have now looked at driving attitudes that increase the risk of accidents. Positive attitudes that help reduce accident risk are:

- a tolerance and consideration for other road users
- a realistic appraisal of your own abilities
- a high degree of care for your own safety and that of your passengers and other road users.

You need to be able to recognise your own limitations and to be able to set aside personal goals in the interests of safety – an example would be restraining yourself from reacting aggressively to another road user's aggressive behaviour. You also need to make decisions carefully, taking full account of the traffic conditions and not acting unpredictably.

Recognise that attitudes affect safety

Understanding your own attitudes and changing them to reduce accident risk is a difficult task. The first stage is to be aware of the effect that your attitudes can have on your driving safety. One way of gaining some insight into this is the use of attitude tests. By answering a few simple questions you can gain some idea of your attitudes and a measure of your accident risk.

Research evidence shows that well-designed attitude tests give an accurate indication of an individual's likely accident rate. The questionnaire on the next page is an example of this type of test. The actual number of accidents for any given driver will depend on many things, but questionnaires of this kind reflect the way that people drive and accurately predict the risk of having an accident.

Check your own attitudes

Use the questionnaire opposite to assess your attitude to driving. Try and be as truthful as possible – the more truthful you are the more accurate the result will be.

If the table shows you to have a high accident risk, you need to think seriously about what you can do to change the attitudes that put you at risk. The next section analyses some of these attitudes and suggests how you might begin to tackle them.

Attitudes to driving

Listed below are some statements about driving. For each one show how far you agree or disagree with it by putting a circle around the appropriate number. For example circling 1 means that you strongly agree with the statement.

	Strongly agree	Agree	Neither agree nor disagree	Disagree	Strongly disagree
Decreasing the speed limit on motorways is a good idea	1	2	(3)	4	5
Even at night time on quiet roads it is important to keep within the speed limit	(1)	2	3	4	5
Drivers who cause accidents by reckless driving should be banned from driving for life	1	2	3	(4)	5
People should drive slower than the limit when it is raining	(1)	2	3	4	5
Cars should never overtake on the inside lane even if a slow driver is blocking the outside lane	1	(2)	3	4	5
Penalties for speeding should be more severe	1	(2)	3	4	5
In towns where there are a lot of pedestrians, the speed limit should be 20 mph	(1)	2	3	4	5

When you have finished you can add up the numbers which you have circled. If you scored less than 15 you tend to agree with the statements. If you scored between 15 and 21 you are generally neutral on average. If you scored more than 21 you tend to disagree with the statements. Drivers who tend to disagree with these statements turn out to have approximately five times the accident risk of those who agree.

Acknowledge resistance to change

Most drivers would accept that developing a safety conscious attitude is important, but a problem exists because we believe our own attitudes are right and are reluctant to accept evidence that we need to change them. Attitude to speed is a key area where there is often resistance to change. To assess your own attitude to speed, complete the questionnaire that follows.

Driving speed

For each question put a circle around the number corresponding to the answer that applies to you during your normal everyday driving (not during emergency driving).

	Never or very infrequently	Quite infrequently	Infrequently	Frequently	Always
How often do you exceed the 70 mph limit during a motorway journey?	1	(2)	3	4	5
How often do you exceed the speed limit in built up areas?	1	2	3	(4)	5
How often do you drive fast?	1	2	3	(4)	5

When you have finished, you can add up the numbers which you have circled. If you scored less than 7, you tend to speed infrequently. If you scored between 7 and 12 you tend to speed a little more frequently. If you scored more than 12 you tend to speed often. Drivers who indicate on this questionnaire that they speed often have about three times the accident risk of those who speed infrequently.

If you have scored more than 12 on the questionnaire do you agree that you have a greater risk of causing an accident? Or do you think there are mitigating circumstances in your case?

If you do think there are mitigating circumstances, make a list of these and then decide whether they are genuinely mitigating or whether they spring from a reluctance to accept change.

Discussing this with a colleague could help to make your assessment more objective.

Many drivers who are fast, aggressive and inconsiderate are quite happy with the way they drive and do not accept that it is unsafe. They tend to think that their behaviour is more common than it really is, and that it is the result of external pressures rather than their own choice. These rationalisations create barriers to attitude change, and need to be challenged to allow scope for change.

Recognise your own vulnerability

If you have inappropriate attitudes towards driving, and are able to acknowledge this, the next step is to identify safety as your primary concern. Consider the elements that bolster your unsafe driving attitudes and how you can change them. Most important amongst these are:

   a false sense of personal invulnerability

   an illusion of control.

These attitudes tend to prevent us from accepting that the risks of driving apply to us as well as to other people.

Critical self-awareness – the key to driving skill

Acknowledging the need to change attitudes is difficult because the evidence is statistical and most people trust their own experience rather than statistics. If you are a fast or aggressive driver, you may not make the connection between your attitudes and the way you drive even if you have been in an accident. Research has shown that drivers have a strong tendency to blame the road conditions or other drivers rather than themselves for the accidents that they cause. This helps to explain why there is a strong tendency for drivers to repeatedly make the same mistakes and become involved in the same kinds of accidents.

A fully professional approach to driving requires you to take an objective look at the facts, to be prepared, where there is evidence, to discard inappropriate attitudes and to develop a critical awareness of your own attitudes and capabilities.

These are key steps to achieving this critical self-awareness:

   acknowledge that attitudes affect driving performance

   be aware of your own attitudes and recognise that they affect your risk of having an accident

   recognise that you are vulnerable

   make safety your primary concern in all your driving decisions

   consider your own experience of near misses or accidents and what you can learn from them

   carry through changes in attitude to your driving performance by applying them in every driving situation.

Concentration and alertness

Concentration and alertness are also key mental aspects of driving skill. This section looks at the factors which can help or hinder them.

Our ability to handle information about the environment is limited. We cope with this by giving more attention to some parts of the environment than others and concentrate on them. This is important in driving because we react most quickly to things happening in the part of the environment on which we are concentrating.

One way of seeing this is to imagine your field of view as a picture – you can see the whole picture but you can only concentrate on one part of it at a time.

If you concentrate your vision on a small area you are less aware of the whole picture.

If you scan different areas of the environment in turn, you become more aware of the picture as a whole.

Scanning the environment

Drivers who can rapidly scan the whole environment looking for different kinds of hazards have a lower risk of accident than drivers who concentrate on one area. There are several ways you can develop your ability to do this:

- move your eyes around and look in all directions
- look for hazards in any shape or size and from any direction
- develop your sensitivity to the variety of possible hazards in different driving situations – this depends on learning, experience and a commitment to developing this awareness.

Looking but not seeing

What we see depends to a large extent on what we expect to see. You may have experienced, at one time or another, pulling out and narrowly missing a bicycle coming from the direction in which you have just looked. Errors of this type are common because drivers are generally looking for cars or lorries but not other road users such as bicycles or motorcycles, which they fail to see. When we concentrate we do not just look at a particular part of a scene, we look for particular types of objects in that scene. We find it easier to detect objects that we expect to see, and react more quickly to them. Conversely, we often fail to see objects that we do not expect to see.

In looking for cars and lorries, drivers can become blind to smaller, less expected road users.

Developing your hazard awareness

Some processing of information goes on at a subconscious level but a prompt can summon our attention to it. An example is the way we prick up our ears when we hear our name mentioned. Experienced drivers rapidly and automatically switch their attention to events happening outside their field of focus because they have a subconscious or instinctive understanding of the implications of particular traffic situations.

In the following chapters of *Roadcraft* we analyse many examples of traffic situations for the hazards that occur in them. You may wonder whether so many examples are necessary, but their purpose is to increase your understanding of the potential hazards in each situation. The aim is to 'pre-sensitise' your awareness so that when you encounter a situation you already know what hazards to look for and can respond to them more quickly.

Alertness

Alertness determines the amount of information you can process – it can be thought of as mental energy and its opposite is tiredness or fatigue. Alertness depends on many things, but with routine tasks like driving, it tends to decrease with time spent on the task. Alertness also depends to some extent on your personality. Extroverts (outgoing people who need a lot of external stimulation) are probably more susceptible to fatigue than introverts (inward looking people who avoid high levels of stimulation).

To drive well we need to remain alert – ready to anticipate, identify and respond to hazards. But most driving is routine, it places few demands on our abilities and the risk of accidents from moment to moment is small. This relatively low level of stimulation makes it easy to lose concentration, and we need to take active steps to maintain it. In busy urban traffic, the demands of driving may be sufficiently stimulating, but on long journeys on motorways or rural roads other forms of stimulation are needed.

Alertness and anxiety

Alertness depends on your level of anxiety and there is an optimum level of anxiety for any task. A small amount of anxiety arising from a sound understanding of the risks involved can help to maintain alertness and readiness to respond. No anxiety at all dampens your responsiveness and decreases your speed of reaction. Too much anxiety can result in failure to process information and respond appropriately.

You can help yourself to stay alert by:

- consciously assessing the current level of risk
- constantly updating your assessment
- talking yourself through the risks of the traffic situation.

If you actively maintain your awareness of the risks in this way, it will help you to keep anxiety at an optimum level, and you will be less likely to neglect a potentially dangerous situation.

Fatigue

The ultimate loss in alertness is falling asleep at the wheel, and it appears to be a significant cause of motorway accidents. Professional drivers need to be aware that fatigue is related to the total time spent at work and not just to the time spent at the wheel. If you are tired from other duties before you start a journey, you are much more at risk from fatigue during the journey. Fatigue is a particular problem for professional drivers because professional and social pressures encourage them to continue driving beyond what they know is their safety limit.

Monotonous conditions

Driving for long periods of time in monotonous conditions such as low-density traffic, fog, at night or on a motorway reduces stimulation and promotes fatigue. Most people experience some fatigue, whatever the conditions, if they drive for longer than about four hours.

How to combat fatigue

Reduce the risk of fatigue by making sure that you are not tired before you start driving. Adjust your seat so that your driving position is comfortable. Bad posture causes muscular fatigue which in turn causes mental fatigue. Emergency driving often causes tension in posture which can also cause fatigue. As far as possible, try to relax your posture during emergency driving.

Night driving puts heavy demands on the eyes and any slight eyesight irregularity can cause stress and fatigue. If you find you are suffering from fatigue unexpectedly, especially at night, it is as well to get your eyes tested. As we age, most of us develop eye irregularities and can benefit from correctly prescribed glasses.

Noise and vibration cause fatigue, so do everything possible to reduce noise in the vehicle. Open windows are a major source of noise so keep them closed and use the ventilation controls instead, but make sure that you have enough ventilation to stay alert.

Taking rest breaks is essential to recover from the onset of fatigue. It appears that most people need a rest break of at least 20 minutes to restore alertness. On long journeys you should plan a series of rest breaks, but recognise that each successive break will give less recovery than the one before. Physical activity helps recovery, so include some walking as well as sitting down and relaxing during planned breaks.

Drivers over 45 need to be aware that they are more at risk of and recover less quickly from fatigue than younger drivers.

Biological rhythms

Alertness is reduced if you drive at times when you would normally be asleep or if you have not had a normal amount of sleep. It also varies with the time of day:

- our reactions tend to be slightly faster in the early evening than in the morning
- there seems to be a dip in alertness after the midday meal
- the greatest risk of fatigue-related accidents is between the hours of midnight and 8.00 a.m.

Irregular work and shift patterns also increase the risk of fatigue.

If you feel drowsy, if your eyelids are heavy and the rear lights ahead start to blur, you must do something to stop yourself falling asleep. Take a rest as soon as it is safe.

Learning skills

Safe driving habits depend on having both appropriate attitudes and appropriate skills in hazard perception and vehicle control. You will find it easier to improve and develop your skills if you have some understanding of how we learn skills and of what role instruction plays in the learning process.

Skilled performance of any task depends on three main elements:

- rapid and accurate perception of the relevant information
- rapid choice of an appropriate response
- accurate execution of the chosen response.

Attitude, as we have seen, is important in identifying what is relevant and in selecting what is appropriate. Speed and accuracy, the other attributes of skill, depend on practice and feedback.

Practice and feedback

The two basic requirements for skill development are practice and feedback on the effect of our actions. The better the feedback the better the learning. Complicated skills, such as driving, are built up from smaller skill elements. Early in practice we need detailed feedback on each of the elements but later, as the different elements of a skill are put together and become automatic, we are less and less aware of our individual actions. This has two results: firstly, each decision covers a bigger task so that fewer decisions are needed; and secondly, our actions become smoother and less hurried.

When you have mastered the basic controls and skills required to drive a car, you can devote more of your attention to the road and traffic conditions. This improves your anticipation and response to hazards and is what advanced driving is all about. Your performance becomes more relaxed and efficient, making it appear that you have all the time in the world.

Throughout this book you will find many routines, such as the system of car control, designed to improve your driving. At first they will put heavy demands on your attention and thinking time, but as you get used to them, they will become second nature. Learning *Roadcraft* skills mirrors the process by which you learnt the basic driving skills to pass your test. At first manoeuvres like changing gear or doing a multi-point turn required all your attention, but with practice they became automatic, allowing you to devote more of your attention to reading the road.

There is a possible negative side to this, especially if you tend to think of driving as a mainly mechanical activity. Once a routine has been learnt, performance can become rigid and unable to respond to changing circumstances. We have already touched on this resistance to learning from experience, and it is something you need to be aware of when evaluating new approaches to old problems.

Instruction

Driver training at basic and advanced levels can accelerate your learning, enabling you to develop skills that you might otherwise never possess. Training can improve your hazard perception by making you aware of the potentially dangerous situations in different traffic environments, and by giving you practice in detecting them. But it is important for you to take an active role in developing your own learning. We each learn differently, and you alone can identify which methods work best for you. To learn effectively you need to have the right balance between instruction and practice. Instruction can draw your attention to parts of a task or ways of doing things but practice is the only way in which skills become automatic and readily available when you need them.

Overconfidence after training

In the period following training, drivers can get into serious difficulties because they overestimate their new abilities. On finishing a well-supervised course your driving ability and your confidence should be in balance. As you practise the methods you have learnt there is a possibility of a mismatch developing between your actual driving ability and the confidence you have in it. There is then a danger that your confidence will take you into situations which you cannot handle, and which might result in an accident. Recognise that this is a problem you will have to tackle whenever you learn new skills. Observe your own driving critically and drive within your known limits. Try to keep your confidence in your ability and your actual ability in balance.

The following chapters explain techniques of vehicle control that can help to increase your safety and reduce your risk of having an accident, but they can only do this if they are supported by positive attitudes, concentration and above all critical self-awareness.

Review

In this chapter we have looked at:

the risks of having an accident

the failure of drivers to learn from experience

the characteristics of a good driver

how your attitudes affect your driving

how to recognise and cope with red mist

practical steps towards changing unsafe attitudes

alertness, concentration and the problem of fatigue

how to develop your driving skills.

Check your understanding

What are the four types of driver that have a higher than average accident risk?

Do drivers who have had an accident generally alter their driving as a result?

What are the attitudes that predispose you to risk?

Why are drivers who suffer from red mist at higher risk of having an accident?

What can drivers do to avoid red mist?

What can you do to stay alert?

What can you do to combat fatigue?

How do we learn new skills?

If you have difficulty in answering any of these questions, look back over the relevant part of this chapter to refresh your memory.

The system of car control

The need for a system of car control

This chapter explains the system of car control, and shows you how to use the system to negotiate hazards. A feature of nearly all road accidents is driver error. The purpose of the system of car control is to prevent accidents by providing an approach to hazards which is safe, systematic, simple and applicable in all circumstances. If you use it consistently with the right frame of mind, good observation and a high level of skill in vehicle control, you should avoid causing accidents yourself and be able to anticipate many of the hazards caused by other road users.

Using the system will help to give you calm control of your vehicle, and enable you to deal with hazards without getting flustered. Your progress will be steady and unobtrusive – the characteristics of a skilled driver.

Driving skills

Driving requires more than pure handling skills. Many hazards encountered by drivers are unpredictable. You need an investigative approach to recognise and negotiate them safely. Driving uses both mental and physical skills:

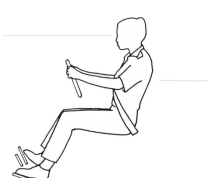

Mental skills

The ability to scan the environment, recognise relevant dangers or hazards, decide on their priority and form an achievable driving plan.

Physical skills

The ability to translate intentions and thoughts into physical action accurately and smoothly.

In using these skills you need to take into account:

- real ability as opposed to perceived ability (what you can actually do as opposed to what you think you can do – in the average driver there is a significant gap between real and perceived ability and a key objective of driver training is to bring perceptions in line with reality)
- the capabilities of the vehicle
- the prevailing weather and road conditions.

Drivers have a great deal to think about and anticipate; road and traffic conditions continually change, requiring you to make frequent adjustments of course and speed. You need to take into account the activities of other road users and what they might do, the closeness of other vehicles, the need to signal intentions, the road and surface conditions, the weather, and how your vehicle is handling. The system of car control simplifies these tasks. It provides a simple and consistent method of driving which ensures that you overlook no detail and leave nothing to chance.

The system of car control gives you that essential aspect of safe driving – time to react.

Hazards

A hazard is anything which is potentially dangerous. A hazard can be immediate and obvious, such as a car approaching you on the wrong side of the road, or it may be less obvious but just as potentially dangerous, such as a blind bend which conceals a lorry reversing into your path. Much of the skill of *Roadcraft* is in recognising hazards – the situations that are potentially dangerous – and then taking the appropriate action to cope with them. One of the main causes of accidents is the failure to recognise hazardous situations. If you fail to see the possible danger you cannot take actions to avoid it.

See Chapter 1,
Becoming a better driver
and Chapter 3,
Observation.

On the roads you will meet three main types of hazard:

- physical features such as junctions, roundabouts, bends or hill crests
- risks arising from the position or movement of other road users
- problems arising from variations in the road surface, weather conditions and visibility.

At the end of your next journey, look back over the way you approached and negotiated hazards and ask yourself the following questions.

Did you always know what was happening behind before changing direction or speed? Were you always in the right gear for the hazard?

Were you able to negotiate all the hazards smoothly without any snatched last-minute adjustments?

How good are you at identifying situations that are potentially dangerous? Next time you drive along a route you use regularly – say your normal route to work – examine the route carefully for situations that are potentially dangerous and where in the past you have not used sufficient caution. Plan how you will negotiate each of these situations in future.

The system of car control

The system of car control is a way of approaching and negotiating hazards that is methodical, safe and leaves nothing to chance. It promotes careful observation, early anticipation and planning, and a systematic use of the controls to achieve maximum vehicle stability. It is a systematic way of dealing with an unpredictable environment. It is central to *Roadcraft*, drawing together all other driving skills in a co-ordinated response to road and traffic conditions. It gives you the time to select the best position, speed and gear to negotiate the hazards safely and efficiently.

Driving hazards come singly and in clusters; they overlap and change all the time. The system accommodates this continual fluctuation by means of a centrally flexible element – you, the driver. As with the other skills in *Roadcraft* you have responsibility for using the system actively and intelligently. When you use the system to approach and negotiate a hazard you consider and use a logical sequence of actions to take you past it safely and efficiently. If new hazards arise, you adapt by reassessing the situation and reapplying the system at an appropriate phase.

The five phases of the system

The system is divided into five phases:

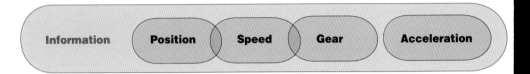

Each phase is dependent on the one before, and you should consider the phases in sequence. Normally you would start by considering your information needs, and then work through each phase in turn. But if road conditions change, you need to consider new information and re-enter the system at an appropriate phase, continuing through it in sequence. The system must be used flexibly in response to actual road conditions; do not follow the sequence rigidly if it is inappropriate to the circumstances.

The phases of the system cover all the points you need to consider on the approach to a hazard. At each phase there are a number of points to consider, but you should only apply those points that are relevant to the situation.

The importance of the information phase

Taking, using and giving information introduces the system, and continues throughout it. You always need to be seeking information to plan your driving and you should provide information whenever other road users could benefit from it. Information allows you to adapt the system to changes in road circumstances, and so continuous assessment of information overlaps with and runs through all the other phases of the system. It is the framework on which the other phases – position, speed, gear, acceleration – depend.

Continuous assessment of information runs through every phase of the system.

Use of the horn

Sound your horn whenever you think another road user could benefit. The purpose of the horn is to inform others that you are approaching and give them time to react. It gives you no right to proceed, and should never be used as a rebuke. It can be used at any stage of the system.

See Chapter 6, Driver's signals.

Mirrors and signals

Constantly assess the situation ahead and to the side for changes in the circumstances. Use your mirrors as often as is necessary to be fully aware of what is happening behind you. Give a signal whenever it could benefit another road user but do not signal if no one else will benefit.

At certain points in the system specific checks for information are important. **Before you change course or speed you need to know what is happening in front, to the sides and behind you; mirror checks at these points are essential.** Remember the *Highway Code* advice of mirrors–signal–manoeuvre, even though you may at times decide a signal is not necessary.

The phases of the system are set out on the next page. The diagram explains the key features of the system, and includes cross references to other chapters. These cross references are necessary for a complete understanding of the system, and need to be read in conjunction with it. Other chapters give a full treatment of the different skills called on when you use the system. When and how you read them depends on your own study plan. If you are using *Roadcraft* as part of a course, ask your instructor for advice.

If you fail to consider information at every phase, and especially before you change speed or direction, the system will not work.

The system of car control

Information

Position

The information phase overlaps every other phase of the system.

Take information
Look all round you. Scan to the front and sides. **Use your mirrors at the appropriate points in the system.**

See Chapter 3, Observation.

Use information
Using the information you have gathered, plan how to deal with the identified hazards and make contingency plans for dealing with the unexpected. Decide on your next action using the system as a guide. If new hazards arise consider whether you need to re-run the system from an earlier phase.

See Chapter 3, Observation, page 34, Planning.

Give information
If you have decided a signal could help other road users, give it; remember other road users include pedestrians and cyclists. Your options include indicators, arm signals, sounding your horn and flashing your lights. Sound your horn whenever it could benefit other road users, no matter what stage of the system you are at. Generally the earlier the warning the greater the benefit.

See Chapter 6, Driver's signals.

Position yourself so that you can pass the hazard/s safely and smoothly.

See Chapter 7, Positioning.

Take account of other road users, including pedestrians, cyclists and children.

Continuo

Speed | Gear | Acceleration

Speed

djust your speed as ecessary. Use the ccelerator, brake or when necessary to void skidding) ears to give you the peed which will nable you to omplete the anoeuvre. Make ood use of cceleration sense.

ee Chapter 4, cceleration, using gears, raking and steering and hapter 11, Speed and afety.

im to make all djustments in peed smoothly and teadily; early nticipation is ssential for this.

Gear

Once you have the right speed for the circumstances, engage the correct gear for that speed.

If you have to brake to get the right speed, you can make the gear change before the end of the braking. But always avoid late braking and snatched gear changes.

See Chapter 4, Acceleration, using gears, braking and steering, page 55.

Acceleration

Taking account of your speed, other road users, and the road and traffic conditions ahead, decide whether it is appropriate to accelerate away from the hazard.

Choose an appropriate point to accelerate safely and smoothly; adjust the amount of acceleration to the circumstances.

See Chapter 4, Acceleration, using gears, braking and steering, page 55.

> *Brake/gear overlap, when used, should always be part of a planned approach that is the most appropriate for the circumstances.*

essment of information runs through every phase of the system.

Use the system flexibly

The key point to remember is that the system depends on your using it intelligently and responsively. It is not an automatic mechanism but has to be adapted by you to the circumstances that arise. Used intelligently, it provides a logical but flexible sequence for dealing with hazards:

- you should consider all the phases of the system on the approach to every hazard, but you may not need to use every phase in a particular situation
- the information phase spans the whole system and entails a constant reassessment of plans
- if a new hazard arises consider whether you need to return to an earlier phase of the system.

Once you have learnt the system, practise it continually. It will become second nature, forming the basis upon which the finer points of your driving can be built.

We shall now look at how the system is applied to three of the commonest hazards: a right-hand turn, a left-hand turn and a roundabout.

Practise applying the system

Familiarise yourself with the five phases of the system and practise working through them whenever you drive. Remember to use the system flexibly according to the circumstances.

At first it might help to name each phase out loud as you enter it.

Review your performance and identify whether you:

- consider each phase
- consider all the aspects of each phase
- are systematic in working through the phases.

Where you have identified problems, work through them one by one, solving the first problem before you go on to the next.

Applying the system to a right-hand turn

Information

Throughout this manoeuvre use your mirrors and look to the front and sides to gather information on the position and intentions of other road users. Consider giving signals or sounding your horn at any point where they can benefit other road users. Remember these include pedestrians as well as cyclists and drivers.

At all times know what is going on all around you, and let other road users know what you intend to do. Taking, using and giving this information is essential before you change speed or direction.

Position

Move on to the appropriate course to make the manoeuvre in good time. Generally this will be towards the centre of the road, but pay attention to:

● the width of the road

● any lane markings

● obstructions in the road

● the speed, size and position of other traffic

● the flow of following traffic

● getting a good view

● making your intentions clear to other road users.

Speed

Adjust your speed as necessary. Use the accelerator or brake to give you the speed which will enable you to complete the manoeuvre. Make good use of acceleration sense. Know and follow the *Highway Code* advice on road junctions.

Gear

Once you have the right speed for the circumstances, engage the correct gear for that speed.

See Chapter 4, Acceleration, using gears, braking and steering.

Acceleration

Choose the appropriate point to accelerate safely and smoothly away from the hazard with due regard to the amount of acceleration, the nature of the road and road surface, traffic conditions ahead, and the position and movement of other road users.

Applying the system to a left-hand turn

Information

Throughout this manoeuvre use your mirrors and look to the front and sides to gather information on the position and intentions of other road users. Consider giving signals or sounding your horn at any point where they can benefit other road users. Remember these include pedestrians as well as cyclists and drivers.

At all times know what is going on all around you, and let other road users know what you intend to do. Taking, using and giving this information is essential before you change speed or direction.

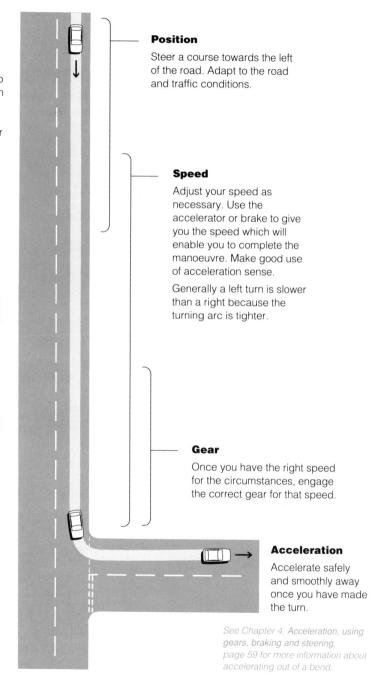

Position

Steer a course towards the left of the road. Adapt to the road and traffic conditions.

Speed

Adjust your speed as necessary. Use the accelerator or brake to give you the speed which will enable you to complete the manoeuvre. Make good use of acceleration sense.

Generally a left turn is slower than a right because the turning arc is tighter.

Gear

Once you have the right speed for the circumstances, engage the correct gear for that speed.

Acceleration

Accelerate safely and smoothly away once you have made the turn.

See Chapter 4, Acceleration, using gears, braking and steering, page 59 for more information about accelerating out of a bend.

Applying the system to a roundabout

Information

Identify hazards. Scan to the front, sides and rear. Use your mirrors and consider an over the shoulder check. Decide early which exit to take and in which lane to approach the roundabout.

Consider whether to signal.

Keep alert for an early view of traffic both on the roundabout and approaching it from other entrances.

As you approach the roundabout be prepared to stop, but look for your opportunity to go.

Position

Your approach course will depend on which exit you intend to take and the number of approach lanes (see *Highway Code*).

Speed

Lose speed smoothly, using either deceleration or brakes. Your approach speed will be determined by the view of the roundabout and the traffic using it.

Plan to stop, but look to go.

Gear

Select the appropriate gear to proceed onto the roundabout. This will depend on your speed and the traffic conditions.

Acceleration

Choose an appropriate gap in the traffic to accelerate safely and smoothly onto the roundabout without disrupting traffic already using it.

Acceleration

Choose the appropriate point to accelerate safely and smoothly away from the hazard.

Position

Move to the left-hand lane in plenty of time for your exit. Check before you move across that your nearside road space is clear.

When you are on the roundabout deal with any new hazards by using the appropriate features of the system.

31

Review

In this chapter we have looked at:

how a systematic approach to hazards can improve your driving

different types of hazards

what the system of car control is and how to apply it

the importance of taking, using and giving information

using the system flexibly.

Check your understanding

What causes road accidents?

How does the system of car control increase the safety of your driving?

What is a hazard, and what are the three main types of hazard that you will meet on the road?

What are the five phases of the system of car control?

Which phase overlaps and runs through all the other phases?

When should you consider giving a signal?

How should you decide which gear to select?

Why is it vital to use the system flexibly?

If you have difficulty in answering any of these questions, look back over the relevant part of this chapter to refresh your memory.

Use this chapter to find out:

why good observation is vital to safe driving

how to use your observations to make a driving plan

why a driving plan is important

how to improve your observation

how to adapt your driving to speed, weather, road surface and night conditions

how to make the best use of road signs and markings.

Chapter 3

Observation

Why you need good observation skills

This chapter looks at observation skills and how to apply them to your driving. The first part of the chapter looks at the link between observation and planning, and shows how good planning enables you to make the fullest use of your observation skills and to increase your driving safety. The second part of the chapter looks at observation skills in detail. It highlights important sources of information in the traffic environment and explains techniques for improving your skill at observing and applying this information.

Observation

'Observation' means using sight, hearing and even smell to gain as much information about conditions as possible. Effective observation is the foundation of good driving. If you do not know something is there you cannot react to it. Careful observation gives you extra time to think and react, and so gives you more control over your driving.

You may occasionally have caught yourself driving absentmindedly, with your mind anywhere but on your driving. You are thinking about the incident you are driving to, your job or something else, and only noticing what is happening immediately in front of you. In this state you are unprepared to deal with a sudden emergency and are quite likely to become a hazard yourself because you are not fully aware of what other road users are doing.

The *Roadcraft* method of driving requires your active attention to your driving all the time. Your ability to take, use and give information and to apply the system of car control depends on your skills of observation and planning.

Planning

Safe and effective driving depends on systematically using the information gained from observation to plan your driving actions.

Use the information gained by observation to form a driving plan:

- anticipate hazards
- order hazards in importance
- decide what to do.

The purpose of the plan is to put you in the right position at the right speed at the right time to negotiate hazards safely and efficiently. As soon as conditions change a new driving plan is required, so effective planning is a continual process of forming and re-forming plans.

The diagram below shows how the three key stages of planning encourage you to interpret and act on your observations:

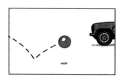 **Observe**

Plan:

 **Anticipate**

 **Order in importance**

 **Decide what to do**

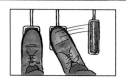 **Act**

We will now look in more detail at the three stages of planning.

Anticipate

The more time that you have to react to a hazard, the more likely that you are able to deal with it safely. Anticipating hazards gives you extra time. Your ability to anticipate depends on your training, your experience and the amount of effort you put in to developing it. A useful technique to help you develop this ability is commenting aloud (making a running commentary as you drive along on what you are observing and how you plan to deal with it).

Start with what you observe and then use your general driving experience to predict how the situation is likely to unfold: for example, your view ahead will often be obscured by vehicles or the layout of the road, yet you know from experience that hazards may be present in the unseen areas. (See the section on observation links at the end of this chapter.) Search the road for clues which might give you added insight into likely developments. To anticipate means to extract the fullest meaning from your observations. For example, when you see a ball bounce into the road you know there is a good chance that children will run after it.

Anticipating the actions of other drivers is important for your own and others' safety. It is unsafe to assume that other drivers will react correctly in any given situation. Observing someone's general progress and road behaviour will give you some idea of what sort of driver they are, but even the most conscientious drivers can make mistakes. Carefully observing other drivers' eye, hand and head movements will give you a better idea of their intentions, but you should always give yourself a safety margin of extra time and space to allow for others' mistakes. If you have a serious accident, being in the right is small consolation.

*Skilful drivers **anticipate** in order to make their plans more effective.*

Order hazards in importance

Among the many observed or anticipated hazards that you identify, you must decide which are significant, and which is the most important. Grade the risks, and deal with them in order of importance. The importance of a hazard may change rapidly, and you must be ready to change your priorities accordingly.

The intensity of danger associated with hazards varies with:

- the hazard itself
- how close it is to you
- road layout
- whether the hazard is stationary or moving
- how fast you are approaching it.

See Chapter 2, The
system of car control,
page 22 .
The greater the element of danger, the higher the priority that you should give it.

Decide what to do

When you have placed the observed and anticipated hazards in order of importance, you are in a position to decide on your course of action. The purpose of your plan is to ensure the safety of yourself and other road users at all times. The appropriate course of action takes account of:

- what can be seen
- what cannot be seen
- what might reasonably be expected to happen
- which hazards represent the greatest threat
- what to do if things turn out differently from expected (contingency plans).

If you plan your driving you should be able to make decisions in a methodical way at any moment and without hesitation. While you are driving you should be continuously anticipating, placing hazards in order of importance and deciding what to do. At first you might find it difficult to consciously work through these three stages all the time, but with practice this will become second nature and prove a quick and reliable guide to action.

Generally things do not just happen, they take a while to develop – good planning depends on early observation and early anticipation of risk.

Throughout your next journey, aim to apply the three stages of planning:

- ● anticipate
- ● order hazards in importance
- ● decide what to do.

During your journey monitor your performance. How successful are you at planning? On how many occasions are you simply reacting to events rather than anticipating them?

Grading a hazard in terms of risk

The chart below shows five different risk situations.

	Risk scale	Your action
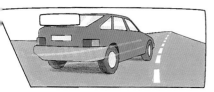	**1** A car pulls out at a junction, turning left and joining your path.	Here the risk is a positive danger requiring drastic action to avoid a collision. Brake hard and move out if possible. No time to sound the horn – in fact the use of the horn may be counter-productive. The driver of the car may brake.
	**2** A car is stationary at the junction and angled to turn left. The driver has not looked in your direction. The brake lights go off and the car begins to move.	This situation contains serious risk. Alter your position if you have not already done so and lose speed sharply. Make a long horn note.
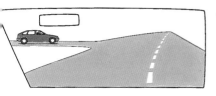	**3** A car is on its final approach to the junction, slowing as if to stop, but you do not have eye contact with the driver.	The driver of the car is unaware of your presence. The risk is a real one. The driver may pull out. Alter your course to maximise the distance between you and the other car, and alter your speed. Consider a short horn note.
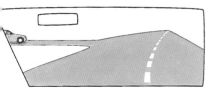	**4** A car comes into view approaching the junction from the left.	The presence of the car represents a slight risk. Consider altering your position and speed.
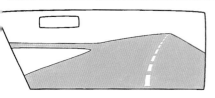	**5** Road junction is free of traffic.	Every road junction poses a risk. This junction is clear and vision is good. No action is required other than to keep making vision scans until the potential risk passes.

Improving your observation skills

We shall now look at ways of developing observational skills.
We start by looking at how you actually use your eyes.

Use your eyes – scanning

Use your eyes to build up a picture of what is happening all
around you, as far as you can see, in every direction. The best
way to build this picture is to use your eyes in a scanning motion
which sweeps the whole environment: the distance, the mid-
ground, the foreground, the sides and rear. Drivers who scan the
environment looking for different kinds of hazard have a lower
risk of accidents than drivers who concentrate only on one area,
so develop the habit of scanning repeatedly and regularly.

Scanning is a continuous process. When a new view opens out in
front of you, quickly scan the new scene. By scanning the whole
of the environment you will know where the areas of risk are.
Check and recheck these risk areas in your visual sweeps. Avoid
staring at particular risk areas because this stops you placing
them in the broader context. Use all your mirrors, and consider
an over the shoulder check on the occasions when it is not safe
to rely on your mirrors alone – for example, when reversing,
moving off from the kerb, joining a motorway or leaving a
roundabout.

Routine scanning enables
you to spot all areas of risk,
which you should then check
and re-check.

Peripheral vision

Peripheral vision is the area of eyesight surrounding the central area of sharply defined vision. Learn to react to your peripheral vision as well as your central vision. The eye's receptors in this area are different from the central receptors, and are particularly good at sensing movement. This helps to alert us to areas that need to be examined more closely. Peripheral vision gives us our sense of speed and lateral position, registers the movement of other road users and acts as a cue for central vision.

How speed affects observation

At 70 mph the shortest distance that you can stop in is 96 metres (315 feet). This is approximately the distance between motorway marker posts (100 metres). To anticipate events at this speed you need to be scanning everything between your vehicle and the horizon.

See Chapter 4, page 67, The safe stopping distance rule.

The faster you go the further ahead you need to look. As your speed increases you need consciously to look beyond the point where your eyes naturally come to rest, to allow yourself sufficient time to react.

Fatigue also limits your ability to see at speed. When you are tired you should slow down and consider whether to take a rest and get some fresh air.

Speed increases the distance you travel before you can react to what you have seen, and you need to build this into your safe stopping distance.

Your ability to take in foreground detail decreases with speed and increases as you slow down. In areas of high traffic density such as town centres, you must slow down to be able to take in all the information necessary to drive safely.

Adjust your speed to how well you can see, the complexity of the situation and the distance it will take you to stop. You must always be able to stop within the distance you can see to be clear.

Zones of visibility

The road around you is made up of different zones of visibility. In some areas your view will be good and in others you will only be able to see what is immediately in front of you. Where your view is restricted, use alternative sources of information, making the most of any glimpses of wider views that you can get. Typical areas with restricted views are junctions in towns and winding lanes in the country.

On the approach to a hazard where the view is restricted, use every opportunity to get more information about the road ahead. Look for the features illustrated here:

open spaces and breaks in hedges, fences and walls on the approach to a blind junction

the curvature of a row of trees or lamp posts

reflections in shop windows

the angle of approaching headlights

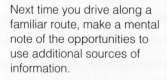

Next time you drive along a familiar route, make a mental note of the opportunities to use additional sources of information.

the angle of shadows cast by headlights and other lights.

Keep your distance

Other vehicles also affect how much you can see. The closer you are to the vehicle in front the less you will be able to see beyond it, especially if it is a van or lorry. In slow-moving traffic it is better to drop back slightly so that you can see what is happening two to three vehicles in front.

When you are following a large lorry you will need to keep well back and take views to both sides of the vehicle.

On motorways it is vital to have a good view of the road ahead because of the speeds involved. Your view will depend on the curvature and gradient of the carriageway, the lane that you are in, the size and position of other vehicles and the height of your own vehicle. Allowing for these, you should keep back far enough from the vehicle in front to maintain a safe following distance. Avoid sitting in the blind spot of other vehicles by moving forward briskly or dropping back. Always check that no one is sitting in your own blind spot before you change lanes.

Do you know exactly where the offside and nearside blind spots are on the vehicles you drive? When you have a safe opportunity sit in the driver's seat and look only through the mirrors. Get a colleague to approach the vehicle from behind. Together work out where the boundaries of the blind spots lie. Then change places and repeat the exercise.

How well do you observe and plan?

Now would be a good time to check whether you actively observe and plan your driving and to begin improving your skills. Next time you drive over an unfamiliar route, run through the questions below before and after your journey, in order to identify your strengths and weaknesses.

Do you constantly observe what is happening:

in the distance?

in the mid-ground?

in front of you?

to the sides of you?

behind you?

Do you anticipate what is likely to happen and adapt your driving accordingly?

Do you rank the hazards you have observed or anticipated in order of importance?

Do you use your observations to plan your actions?

Do you make contingency plans?

Many people relax their concentration when driving along familiar routes, so assess your performance over a routine journey as well.

Keep a record of any weaknesses you identify and repeat these tests at a later date (say in a fortnight) to see how you are progressing. Consider doing this exercise with a colleague, who may be able to give you a more independent assessment of your strengths and weaknesses.

Weather conditions

The weather affects how far you can see, and how your vehicle performs, so it is central to your observation and driving plan. When weather conditions reduce visibility, you should reduce your speed and regularly check your actual speed on the speedometer. You should always be able to stop within the distance you can see to be clear.

Examples of weather conditions which reduce visibility are:

fog and mist

heavy rain

snow and sleet

bright sunshine.

Use of lights in bad weather

Choose your lights according to the circumstances.

Switch on your dipped headlights when visibility is poor in daylight or fading light. This is particularly important in fog or heavy rain in daylight, when sidelights are virtually invisible.

Generally you should use your dipped headlights whenever your wipers are in constant use.

When there is fog or falling snow at night, foglights often give a better view than dipped headlights. Use them as an alternative to or together with dipped headlights.

Switch off your rear foglights when you leave the fog in order not to dazzle following drivers.

Do not use your main headlight beam when you are behind another vehicle in fog – it may dazzle the driver, and will cast a shadow of the vehicle on the fog ahead, disrupting the driver's view.

Remember that the brilliance of rear foglights can mask the brakelights – allow more distance between you and the car in front and aim to brake gently yourself.

Using your auxiliary controls and instruments in bad weather

Make full use of your washers and wipers to keep your windscreen and rear window as clear as possible. When there is a possibility of freezing fog, put freeze-resistant screen wash in the screen wash reservoir. In fog, rain, or snow regularly check your speedometer for your actual speed. You cannot rely on your eyes to judge speed accurately in these conditions. Low visibility distorts your perception of speed.

Observing when visibility is low

When visibility is low, keep to a slow steady pace and use the edge of the carriageway, hazard lines and cat's eyes as a guide, especially when approaching a road junction or corner. Staring into featureless mist tires the eyes very quickly. Focus instead on what you can see: the vehicle in front, the edge of the road or the road ahead. Avoid fixing your focus on the tail lights of the vehicle in front because they will tend to draw you towards it. You could collide if it stopped suddenly. Be ready to use your horn to inform other road users of your presence.

Always be prepared for a sudden stop in the traffic ahead. Do not follow closely, and only overtake other traffic when you can see that it is absolutely safe to do so. This is seldom possible in fog on a two-way road. At junctions when visibility is low, wind down your window and listen for other vehicles, and consider using your horn.

Weather and the road surface

Besides affecting visibility, the weather will also affect the road surface. Snow, rain or ice will greatly reduce the grip of the tyres, making skids and aquaplaning more likely.

See Chapter 5, Skidding.

Be aware that special hazards exist in summer. Dust on the road reduces tyre grip. Rain may produce a slippery road surface especially after a long dry spell.

Micro climates

Ice and wetness can linger in areas of shadow.

Look out for micro climates which can cause frost and wet patches to linger in some areas after they have disappeared elsewhere. Landscape features such as valley bottoms, shaded hillsides and shaded slopes, or large areas of shadow cast by trees or buildings can cause ice to linger and result in sudden skidding. Bridge surfaces are often colder than the surrounding roads because they are exposed on all sides, and can be icy when nearby roads are not. Patchy fog is particularly dangerous and is a common catalyst of multiple pile-ups.

Adapt your driving to the weather conditions

Bad weather is often blamed for causing accidents, but the real cause is inappropriate driving for the conditions that exist. In dense fog, driving at a speed at which you can stop in the distance you can see to be clear means driving so slowly that many trips are not worthwhile. The best way to deal with a skid is not to get into it in the first place. Careful observation, the correct speed and adequate braking distances are crucial for safe driving but they are especially important in difficult weather conditions. Accidents occur when these rules are ignored.

Road surface

The type and condition of the road surface affects tyre grip and vehicle handling characteristics. Tyre grip is fundamental to driving control because it determines steering, acceleration and braking. Most drivers do not pay sufficient attention to this.

Always look well ahead to identify changes in the road surface, and adjust the strength of your braking, acceleration and steering to retain adequate road holding.

Always observe the camber of the road on a curve or bend.

See Chapter 8, page 113, Camber and superelevation.

Surfaces which slope upwards to the inside of the curve make cornering more difficult.

Surfaces which slope downwards to the inside of the curve help cornering.

The surfaces of most roads are good for road holding when they are clean and dry. Snow, frost, ice, rain, oil, moist muddy patches, wet leaves, dry loose dust or gravel can cause tyres to lose grip. At hazards such as roundabouts or junctions, tyre deposit and diesel spillage may make the surface slippery at precisely the point where effective steering, braking and acceleration are needed to negotiate the hazard safely.

Surfacing materials	Grip characteristics	Problems
Tarmac or asphalt	Tarmac or asphalt surfaces give a good grip when they are dressed with stones or chips.	In time they become polished and lose some of their skid resistant properties.
Concrete	Concrete road surfaces often have roughened ribs which give a good skid resistant surface.	Some hold water, which freezes in cold weather and creates a slippery surface which is not easily seen.
Cobbles	Low grip when wet.	Rain increases the likelihood of skidding.

Road surface irregularities

Look out for irregularities in the road surface such as potholes, projecting manhole covers, sunken gullies and bits of debris, which can damage the tyres and suspension. If you can alter your course to avoid them without endangering other traffic, do so. If you cannot, slow down to reduce shock and maintain stability as you pass over them.

The road surface in winter

In winter, the ice or frost covering on road surfaces is not always uniform. Isolated patches remain iced up when other parts have thawed out, and certain slopes are especially susceptible to this. Be on the look out for ice or frost patches, which you can detect by their appearance, by the behaviour of other vehicles and by the sudden absence of tyre noise: tyres travelling on ice make virtually no noise at all. Adjust your driving early to avoid skidding.

Driving through water

Driving at speed through water can sharply deflect the front wheels and cause you to lose control. Extra care is needed at night when it is difficult to distinguish between a wet road surface and flood water. Flood water can gather quickly where the road dips and at the sides of the road in poorly drained low lying areas. Dips often occur under bridges.

As you approach a flooded area you should slow down. Avoid driving through water wherever possible. If part of the road is not flooded, use it if you can. When you have to drive through water, drive through the shallowest part but look out for hidden obstructions or subsidence.

If the road is entirely submerged, stop the vehicle in a safe place and cautiously find out how deep the water is. The depth of water that you can safely drive through depends on how high your vehicle stands off the ground and where the electrical components are positioned. If you decide to drive on follow the steps below.

- Engage first gear and keep the engine running fast by slipping the clutch. This prevents water entering the exhaust pipe. In vehicles with automatic gears, use the footbrake to keep the road speed low while running the engine fast. In vehicles with manual gears, use the handbrake to control the road speed, especially when driving downhill into a ford. Do not attempt this technique in vehicles fitted with transmission brakes.

- Drive through the water at a slow and even speed to avoid making a bow wave.

- When you leave the water continue driving slowly and apply the brakes lightly with the left foot until they grip. Repeat this again after a short while until you are confident that your brakes are working normally.

Night driving

Observing in night conditions (which means anything less than full daylight) is more difficult and yields less information. As the light dwindles, your ability to see the road ahead also declines – contrast falls, colours fade and edges become indistinct.

At night your eyes need all the help you can give them. Windows, mirrors, and the lenses of lights and indicators should all be clean to give the best possible visibility. The slightest film of moisture, grease or dirt on the windows or mirrors will break up light and increase glare, making it harder to distinguish what is going on. The lights should be correctly aligned, and adjusted for the vehicle load. The bulbs should all work and the switching equipment should function properly. Windscreen washers, wipers and de-misters should also be working properly.

Lights

On unlit roads your headlights should be on main beam unless they are dipped because of other road users.

Use dipped headlights:

- in built-up areas when visibility from streetlighting is poor
- in situations when dipped headlights are more effective than the main beam, for example when going round a left-hand bend or at a hump back bridge
- in heavy rain, snow and fog when the falling droplets reflect glare from headlights on full beam.

Dip your headlights to avoid dazzling oncoming drivers, the driver in front or other road users; when you overtake another vehicle, return to full beam when you are parallel with it.

You should always drive so as to be able to stop within the area that you can see to be clear; at night this is the area lit by your headlights unless there is full streetlighting. Even in the best conditions your ability to assess the speed and position of oncoming vehicles is reduced at night, so you need to allow an extra safety margin.

Dazzle

Headlights shining directly into your eyes may dazzle you. This can happen on sharp right-hand bends and steep inclines, and when the lights of oncoming vehicles are undipped or badly adjusted. The intensity of the light bleaches the retinas of your eyes and the bleaching effect can continue for some moments afterwards. During this time you can see nothing, which is clearly dangerous.

To avoid dazzle, look towards the nearside edge of the road. This enables you to keep to your course but does not tell you what is happening in the road ahead, so slow down or stop if necessary. If you are dazzled by undipped headlights, flash your own lights quickly to alert the other driver, but do not retaliate by putting on your full beam. If you did, both you and the other driver would be converging blind. If you suffer temporary blindness, stop and wait until your eyes have adjusted.

Following other vehicles at night

When you follow another vehicle, dip your headlights and allow a sufficient gap so that your lights do not dazzle the driver in front. When you overtake, move out early with your headlights still dipped. If a warning is necessary you can flash your lights instead of using the horn. When you are alongside the other vehicle return to full beam. If you are overtaken, dip your headlights when the overtaking vehicle draws alongside you and keep them dipped until they can be raised without dazzling the other driver.

Information from other vehicles' lights

You can get a great deal of useful information from the front and rear lights of other vehicles; for example, the sweep of the headlights of vehicles ahead approaching a bend can indicate the sharpness of the bend, and the brakelights of vehicles in front can give you an early warning to reduce speed.

There are many times when intelligent use of information given by lights will help your driving.

Reflective studs and markings

Reflective studs and markings are a good source of information
about road layout at night. To get the most out of them you need
to be familiar with the *Highway Code*. Roadside marker posts
reflect your headlights and show you the direction of a curve
before you can see where the actual road goes.

Cat's eyes

Cat's eyes indicate the type of white line along the centre of the
road. Generally the more white paint in the line, the greater the
number of cat's eyes. They are particularly helpful when it is
raining at night and the glare of headlights makes it difficult to see.

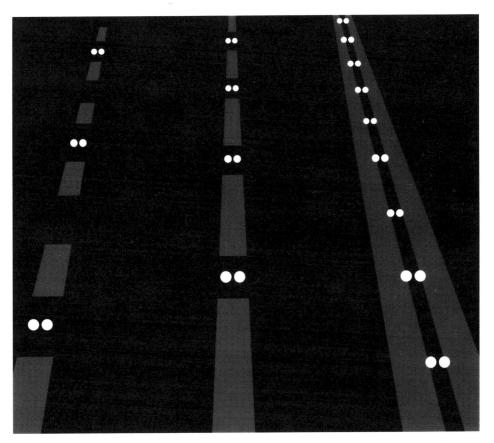

Centre lines:
one cat's eye every
other gap.

Hazard lines:
one cat's eye
every gap.

Double white lines:
twice as many cat's
eyes as hazard lines.

Other ways to improve observation at night

Keep your speed down when you leave brightly lit areas to allow time for your eyes to adjust to the lower level of lighting.

Any light inside the vehicle which reflects off the windows will distract you and reduce your ability to see. In modern vehicles the dials and instruments are positioned and illuminated to avoid this but interior lights, torches, rally lights and cigarette lighters can cause reflections, so you should limit their use as much as possible.

Certain types of spectacles – such as those with tinted lenses and those with photochromatic lenses – may be unsuitable for night driving, so check with your optician.

Night fatigue

Night driving is tiring because it puts extra strain on your eyes, and your body naturally wants to slow down as night draws on. Be aware of this problem and take appropriate action to deal with it. If you are having difficulty keeping your eyes open, you are a danger to yourself and other road users; find somewhere safe to stop, get some fresh air and rest until you are alert enough to continue safely.

See Chapter 1, Becoming a better driver, page 16, Fatigue, for further advice.

Road signs and markings

Road signs and markings provide warnings about approaching hazards, and instructions and information about road use. They need to be incorporated into your driving plan as early as possible. To make the best possible use of road signs and markings you should follow the steps below.

Observe – actively search for road signs and markings in your observation scans, and incorporate the information they give you into your driving plan. Many drivers fail to see and make use of them, and so lose valuable information.

Understand – be able to recognise them immediately. You should be familiar with the current edition of the *Highway Code* and the *Know your Traffic Signs* book. Everyone's memory declines over time, so check your recall of road signs and markings on a regular basis.

React – react to a sign or marking by looking ahead to what it refers to and building the information into your driving plan. Where the sign or marking refers to an unseen hazard, anticipate the hazard and adapt your plan accordingly.

Sometimes you will see several road signs on the same pole. These should generally be read from top to bottom. The nearest event is shown by the top sign, the next nearest event by the sign below that, and so on. Always be careful to use your own observations to link the signs to the road layout ahead.

Unofficial road signs

Make use of unofficial road signs such as 'Mud on Road', 'Car Boot Sale' and 'Concealed Entrance'. They provide additional information and help you anticipate the road conditions ahead.

> Do you always build information from road signs into your driving plan?
>
> When was the last time you looked at road signs in the current *Highway Code*?
>
> Next time you drive, test your observation skills by seeing if you can correctly predict hazards and the road signs warning of them before you actually see the signs.

Local road knowledge

Increasing your local knowledge of the roads can help your driving. Town driving puts heavy demands on your observation, reactions and driving skills, and you need to be alert at all times. At complicated junctions, where it is important to get into the correct lane, local knowledge is a valuable aid. But even when you know the layout of main road junctions, one-way streets, roundabouts and other local features, always plan on the basis of what you can *actually see* – not what usually happens. Inattentiveness is a major cause of accidents and drivers are least attentive on roads they know well. Nine out of ten accidents occur on roads that the driver is familiar with.

Making observation links

Observation links are clues to the likely behaviour of other road users. You should constantly aim to build up your own stock of observation links which will help you anticipate road and traffic conditions. Here are some examples.

When you see...	Look out for...
A cluster of lamp posts 	Probable roundabout ahead.
A single lamp post on its own 	The exit point of a junction.
No gap in a bank of trees ahead 	Road curves to left or right.
Railway line beside road	Road will invariably go over or under it, often with sharp turns.
A pedestrian calls a cab	Cab stopping suddenly or turning or moving away from rank. Pedestrian stepping into the road.
A row of parked vehicles	Doors opening, vehicles moving off. Pedestrians stepping out from behind vehicles. Small children hidden from view.

When you see...	Look out for...
Ice-cream vans, mobile shops, school buses, etc.	Pedestrians, especially children.
A bus at a stop	Pedestrians crossing the road to and from the bus. Bus moving off, possibly at an angle.
Pedal cyclists	Inexperienced cyclist doing something erratic. Cyclist looking over shoulder with the intention of turning right. Strong winds causing wobble. Young cyclist doing something dangerous.
Fresh mud or other deposits on road. Newly mown grass, etc.	Slow-moving vehicles or animals just around the bend.
Post office vans, trade vehicles, etc.	Points where the vehicle may stop, eg post box, shops, public houses, garages, building sites, etc.
Pull-ins, petrol stations, pubs, parking places, etc.	Vehicles moving in and out.
Motorway access points	Vehicles in nearside lane moving out.
Accident	Others slowing down to look.

Write down some of your own observation links in the space provided below.

When you see...   **Look out for...**

Review

In this chapter we have looked at:

observation skills that will help to improve your driving

the link between observation, planning and acting, and the need to anticipate and order hazards in importance

scanning and using peripheral vision to get the maximum information from observation

how speed affects your vision

using additional sources of information when your view is restricted

weather conditions to watch out for and how to adjust your driving to poor visibility

ways of improving observation when you are driving at night

making full use of information from road signs and markings

increasing your skill at making observation links.

Check your understanding

What is the purpose of a driving plan?

What are the three key stages of planning?

How do you use your eyes to get the maximum information about your driving environment?

How can you get more information when your view is restricted?

In what ways does speed affect your vision?

What are the weather conditions that reduce visibility?

When should you switch your headlamps on?

What hazards should you look out for on the road surface?

What are the three steps for building road signs and markings into your driving plan?

Describe at least three examples of observation links.

If you have difficulty in answering any of these questions, look back over the relevant part of this chapter to refresh your memory.

Chapter 4

Acceleration, using gears, braking and steering

Developing your skill at controlling your vehicle

The aim of this chapter is to give you complete control over moving, stopping and changing the direction of your vehicle at all times. To achieve this level of skill you need a good understanding of vehicle controls and how they relate to each other. This chapter looks in detail at the accelerator, gears, brakes and steering and at how to make best use of them.

Although we discuss the controls individually, it is important to understand that in practice they are closely inter-related. They depend for their effectiveness on the grip between the tyres and the road. Your ability to control your vehicle, and the safety of yourself and other road users depend on tyre grip.

The tyre grip trade-off

Your control of the vehicle is totally dependent on the grip between the tyres and the road surface.

There is a limited amount of tyre grip available and this is shared between accelerating, braking and steering forces. If more tyre grip is used for braking or accelerating, there is less available for steering, and vice versa.

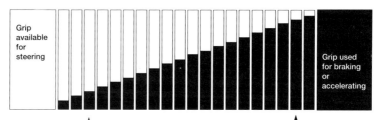

Grip available for steering

Grip used for braking or accelerating

▲ Moderate braking or accelerating leaves plenty of grip for steering

▲ Excessive braking or accelerating leaves little grip for steering

Tyre grip is not necessarily the same on each wheel. It varies with the load on the wheel and this affects how the vehicle handles. Braking, steering and accelerating alter the distribution of the load between the wheels and so affect the vehicle's balance.

Weight distribution

Steady speed	**Accelerating**	**Braking**	**Cornering**	**Cornering and accelerating**	**Cornering and braking**
weight is evenly distributed	weight shifts to the back	weight shifts to the front	weight shifts to the outside of the curve	weight shifts to the outside of the curve and to the back	weight shifts to the outside of the curve and to the front

Braking or accelerating as you go round a corner or bend reduces the amount of control you have over your vehicle. If more tyre grip is used for accelerating or braking, there is less available for steering and this reduces your control over the positioning of your vehicle. Eventually, if there is not enough tyre grip for steering, a skid will develop. The more slippery the road surface, the earlier this will happen. The exact outcome depends on the balance of the vehicle, and whether it has front, back or four wheel drive.

Develop your awareness of tyre grip

As you drive round bends in the next few days, analyse what is happening to your tyre grip in terms of the trade-off between accelerating or braking on the one hand and steering on the other. Ask yourself the following questions:

Do you finish braking before you go into a bend?

Do you avoid accelerating harshly while driving round bends?

The more you brake or accelerate, the less you will be able to steer.

Using the accelerator

If you are in the right gear, depressing the accelerator will increase engine speed. If you are in a gear that is too high for your speed, the engine will not be able to respond because the load from the wheels is too great. Changing to a lower gear reduces the load from the wheels and the engine is able to speed up and so move the vehicle faster.

When the accelerator pedal is released the opposite effect – deceleration – occurs. The engine speed slows down and cylinder compression slows the vehicle down. The lower the gear the greater the slowing effect of the engine (because there are more compression strokes for each rotation of the wheels).

So, in the appropriate gear, the accelerator pedal has two effects:

increase in speed when the pedal is depressed

decrease in speed when the pedal is released.

Acceleration and vehicle balance

Acceleration alters the distribution of weight between the wheels of the car. When a vehicle accelerates the weight is lifted from the front and pushed down on the back wheels. During deceleration the opposite happens. This alters the relative grip of the front and rear tyres.

During acceleration

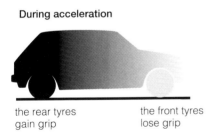

the rear tyres
gain grip

the front tyres
lose grip

During deceleration

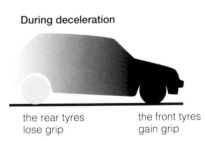

the rear tyres
lose grip

the front tyres
gain grip

How acceleration affects different vehicles

Acceleration affects rear wheel drive, and most four wheel drive vehicles, differently from front wheel drive vehicles.

Front wheel drive vehicles lose grip or traction on their driving wheels because acceleration transfers weight, and therefore grip, from the front wheels to the back wheels. This reduces their ability to accelerate. In severe cases wheel spin occurs. Harsh acceleration or a slippery road surface increases the risk of wheel spin, which can be particularly dangerous when pulling out at a junction. Avoid over accelerating, and only depress the accelerator very gently in slippery conditions.

Rear wheel drive vehicles gain extra grip on their driving wheels, which assists acceleration (but note that *excessive* acceleration will cause the driving wheels to lose traction). At the same time the front is lightened.

Four wheel drive vehicles vary in how the power is divided between the front and back wheels, and in the type of central differential they have. The effects of acceleration therefore vary according to the model but generally four wheel drive vehicles have good grip when accelerating. For precise details consult your vehicle manufacturer.

Developing your skill at using the accelerator

Jerky acceleration is uncomfortable for the passengers, puts unnecessary strains on the vehicle, and adversely affects tyre grip. Use the accelerator deftly, making precise and smooth movements to depress or release it. Thin soled shoes help you to do this.

Acceleration capability varies widely between vehicles and depends on the size of the engine, its efficiency and the power-to-weight ratio. Take time to become familiar with the acceleration capability of any vehicle you drive: the safety of many manoeuvres, particularly overtaking, depends on your good judgement of it.

Always consider the safety implications of accelerating. Sudden sharp movements of the accelerator reduce tyre grip and jeopardise steering control. The faster you go the further you will travel before you can react to a hazard. It will take you longer to stop and, if you crash, your impact speed will be higher.

Acceleration sense

Acceleration sense is the ability to vary vehicle speed in response to changing road and traffic conditions by accurate use of the accelerator. It is used in every driving situation: moving off, overtaking, complying with speed limits, following other vehicles and negotiating hazards. Good acceleration sense requires careful observation, full anticipation, sound judgement of speed and distance, driving experience and an awareness of a particular vehicle's capabilities. A lack of acceleration sense causes many common mistakes: for example, accelerating hard away from a junction and then having to brake sharply to slow to the speed of the vehicles in front; or accelerating to move up behind a slower moving vehicle and then having to brake before overtaking. If you have good acceleration sense you are able to avoid unnecessary braking.

Always comply with the basic driving safety rule: Be able to stop on your own side of the road within the distance you can see to be clear.

When you have the opportunity, drive along a regular route using acceleration sense rather than braking. Notice how it improves your anticipation and increases the smoothness of the drive.

Accelerating on bends

A moving vehicle is at its most stable when its weight is evenly distributed, its engine is just pulling without increasing road speed, and it is travelling in a straight line. Accelerating to increase the road speed round a bend upsets these conditions.

If you accelerate hard and alter direction at the same time you run the risk of demanding too much from the available tyre grip. If the tyres lose grip you lose steering control. To get maximum steering control, you should avoid altering your road speed at the same time.

As soon as a vehicle turns into a bend it starts to slow down and lose stability, due to cornering forces. If you maintain the same accelerator setting as you go into and round a bend you will lose road speed.

See Chapter 8,
Cornering, page 110,
Cornering forces.

To maintain constant speed round the bend and retain stability you need to increase power by depressing the accelerator. How much to depress the accelerator is a matter of judgement but **your purpose is to maintain constant speed, not to increase it**. Increasing road speed on bends reduces vehicle stability.

When you need to steer and increase speed together, use the

accelerator gently. Use extra care in slippery conditions or you will get wheel spin, loss of steering control and a skid.

Acceleration reduces the ability to corner because it shifts the vehicle's weight on to the back wheels and reduces front tyre grip. In front wheel drive vehicles there is a risk of wheel spin on the front wheels because they are the driving wheels. Do not make the mistake of applying even more steering which may lead to an eventual loss of control.

Follow the guiding safety principle and adjust your speed when going round bends so that you can always stop on your own side of the road within the distance you can see to be clear.

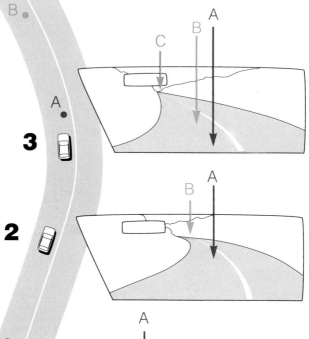

Coming out of the bend

Your new road view (B – C) begins to open rapidly, and is greater than the distance you have travelled (2 – 3). It is safe to accelerate smoothly into the straightening road.

Entering the bend

Your increased road view (A – B) is no greater than the distance you have travelled (1 – 2) so maintain a steady speed.

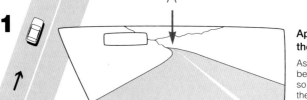

Approaching the bend

As you approach the bend, adjust your speed so that you can stop in the distance you can see to be clear (1 – A)

The key points to remember are:

- select your speed for a bend according to the overall stopping distance
- maintain a constant speed round the bend
- the harder you accelerate, the less your steering ability
- use the accelerator smoothly – jerkiness causes tyre slip
- watch out for slippery surface conditions, and adjust your speed.

Using the gears

The way you use your gears can make or mar your driving. Skilful use of the gears depends on accurately matching the gear to the road speed, and using the clutch and accelerator precisely. Your vehicle can only increase speed if the engine can deliver the power. It can only do this if you are in the right gear. You should aim to:

- be in the correct gear for every road speed and traffic situation
- make all gear changes smoothly
- engage a chosen gear without going through an intermediate gear first
- know the approximate maximum road speed for each gear of the vehicle.

To make rapid progress you should accelerate up to the engine's peak performance point and then change to a higher gear. You therefore need to know the manufacturer's peak engine performance recommendations for your vehicle. This may differ from both the maximum torque and the maximum revs obtainable from the engine.

It is useful to understand how the gears work as this will help you get the most out of them. The main effect of the gears is to transform speed of turning into power of turning and vice versa.

- The bottom gear produces plenty of power but relatively little speed
- The top gear produces plenty of speed but at relatively low power.

The gears in between produce varying combinations of power and speed. To climb a steep hill the road wheels need plenty of power, which is gained at the expense of speed by selecting a low gear. Cruising on a level stretch of motorway requires speed but relatively little power: speed is gained at the expense of power by selecting a high gear.

To gain speed quickly, select a lower gear. This has more power to drive the vehicle along faster. This is because the engine can only increase its speed if the load on it is not too great. A lower gear supplies more power to the wheels and so reduces the load on the engine. But the top speed of a lower gear is limited and eventually you have to change to a higher gear to gain more speed: power is converted into speed.

The greater turning power of low gears also affects tyre grip. The higher the turning power, the more likely tyre slip becomes. This is why it is advisable to use a higher gear when moving slowly in slippery conditions such as on snow, ice or mud. It is also why tyre slip occurs when you accelerate hard in first gear.

Moving off from stationary

The ideal way to move off from a standing start is to accelerate smoothly and to gather speed by steadily working up through the gears. Maximum acceleration through the gears should only be used on occasions of pressing need, and when the road surface and other conditions are right. Over accelerating in low gears or remaining in a gear beyond the limits of its optimum performance damages the engine, uses excessive fuel and results in slower progress. Some engines cut out or misfire if excessively revved and this could be dangerous.

These are the key points which will help you to make skilful use of the gears:

   develop good coordination of hand and foot movements

   recognise when to change gear by the sound of the engine

   choose the right gear for the road speed

   use the brakes rather than engine compression to slow the vehicle (except during hill descents and when there is a risk of skidding)

   brake in good time to slow to the right road speed as you approach a hazard, and then select the appropriate gear

   match engine speed to road speed before you change down.

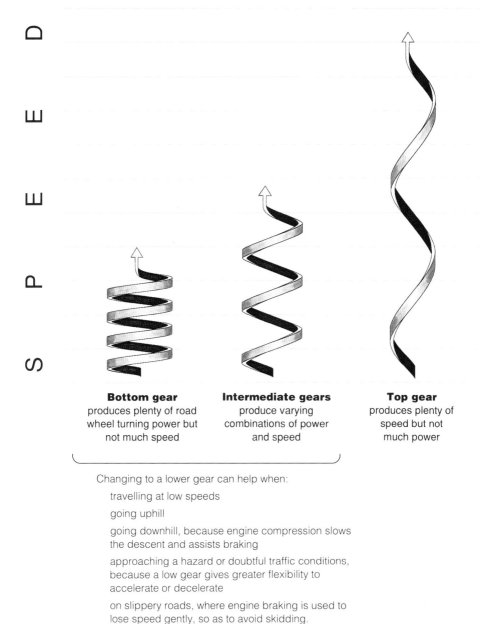

S P E E E D

Bottom gear
produces plenty of road
wheel turning power but
not much speed

Intermediate gears
produce varying
combinations of power
and speed

Top gear
produces plenty of
speed but not
much power

Changing to a lower gear can help when:

travelling at low speeds

going uphill

going downhill, because engine compression slows
the descent and assists braking

approaching a hazard or doubtful traffic conditions,
because a low gear gives greater flexibility to
accelerate or decelerate

on slippery roads, where engine braking is used to
lose speed gently, so as to avoid skidding.

High gears are good for:

cruising at speed

certain slippery conditions where lower
gears may cause wheel spin.

Automatic gearboxes

An automatic gearbox allows you more time to concentrate on your driving and to keep both hands on the steering wheel for longer. Automatic gearboxes operate and behave differently from manual gearboxes and from each other. You need to be familiar with and understand the manufacturer's instructions for any automatic vehicles that you drive. These are the key points to remember:

- always ensure that the footbrake is on before engaging either D or R from stationary
- do not engage D or R with a high revving engine – the choke often causes high revs.

Overlapping braking and gear changing

Sometimes it is helpful to overlap braking with the gear change. Do this by braking normally and changing the gear towards the end of braking. The advantages of this are that it takes less time, contributes to vehicle stability and is often safer because your progress matches the expectations of other road users.

These advantages have to be weighed against the disadvantage that for part of the braking period both hands are not on the steering wheel, and the possibility that the technique could lead to late, excessive braking and rushed gear changes. If you use this technique it must be properly incorporated into your planning. Braking late and rushing a gear change because of inadequate planning can destabilise your vehicle at exactly the point where you need greatest stability to negotiate the hazard.

How well do you use your gears? Ask yourself the following questions as you drive.

Are you always in the right gear?

Do you adjust your road speed first, then select the appropriate gear?

Do you avoid using your gears to slow down except on hills and slippery surfaces?

Do you ever find yourself changing gear halfway round a corner?

You should generally avoid changing gear while cornering because it destabilises the vehicle and requires you to take one hand off the steering wheel.

Examples of situations where brake/gear overlap may be appropriate:

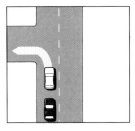

low speed turns into left
and right junctions with a
vehicle close behind

sharp right/left turns
with a vehicle close
behind

going downhill

Slowing down and stopping

You need to be able to slow down or stop your vehicle with it
fully under control. The smoothness of a drive is greatly
improved by early anticipation of the need to slow down or stop,
and by braking gently and progressively. The ability to accurately
estimate the required braking distance at different speeds and in
different conditions is a central skill of safe driving, and one
which you should strive to develop. There are two ways of
slowing down or stopping:

- decelerating (releasing the accelerator pedal)
- using the brakes.

Deceleration

When you release the accelerator the engine slows and through
engine compression exerts a retarding force on the wheels. This
causes the engine to act as a brake, reducing road speed
smoothly and gradually with little wear to the vehicle.

The loss of road speed is greater when you decelerate in a low
gear. (This applies equally to automatic gearboxes.)
Deceleration, or engine braking, provides a valuable way of
losing speed on slippery roads. If the accelerator is released
gently, it provides a steady and smooth braking effect in
conditions where normal braking might lock the wheels – for
example, on slippery roads. Engine braking is also useful on long
descents in hilly country, but for normal driving it is inadequate
for more than gradual variations in speed.

Using the brakes

Use the brakes if you need to make more than a gradual adjustment in road speed. You should generally keep both hands on the wheel while you brake, and plan to avoid braking on bends and corners. You can apply pressure to the footbrake to achieve the slightest check, or until all the wheels lock up (or, where fitted, the antilock braking system intervenes). Always check the effectiveness of the brakes in the vehicles you drive, and make allowances for extra loads or changes in road surface.

Testing your brakes

Every time you use your vehicle you should check that the brakes are working. Check them when the vehicle is stationary before you move off, and check them again when the vehicle is moving.

The stationary test. Check that the brake pedal moves freely and gives a firm positive pressure. Check that the handbrake fully secures the wheels.

The moving test. Make sure that the brake system is working efficiently under running conditions. Test the footbrake as soon as possible after moving off. You only need to do this test once if you are in the same vehicle all day, provided you have no reason to suspect the performance of the brakes. Always consider the safety and convenience of other road users before you do a moving test.

Normal braking

Braking should normally be progressive and increased steadily.

Gently take up the initial free movement of the pedal

Increase the pressure progressively as required

Relax pedal pressure as unwanted road speed is lost

Release the pedal just before stopping to avoid a jerking halt

Braking, tyre grip and balance

Braking reduces the ability to steer because of its combined effects on tyre grip and vehicle balance. Braking moves the weight of the vehicle forward on to the front wheels. This makes the steering heavier and at the same time reduces the grip of the rear tyres. On a bend this reduces stability and can cause the back wheels to lock and go into a rear wheel skid. The harsher the braking, the greater the tyre slip and the less the ability to steer. In slippery conditions harsh braking almost inevitably results in a skid.

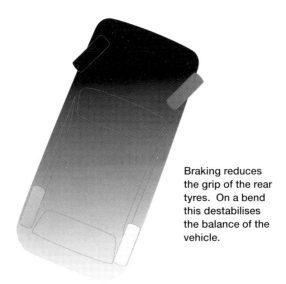

Braking reduces the grip of the rear tyres. On a bend this destabilises the balance of the vehicle.

The safe stopping distance rule

This is one of the guiding principles of *Roadcraft* and should always be observed. By relating your speed to the distance in which you can stop, it enables you to assess the safety of your speed in any situation.

Never drive so fast that you cannot stop comfortably on your own side of the road within the distance you can see to be clear.

The importance of this rule for your own and other people's safety cannot be overstated. It provides a guide to the speed at which you should corner, and it indicates the speed and distance you should keep from other vehicles in all other traffic conditions. Successfully applying this rule requires skill. You need to be aware of:

- the braking capabilities of your vehicle
- the type and condition of the road surface – in slippery or wet conditions braking distances increase greatly
- the effects of cornering, braking and vehicle balance on tyre grip.

The only variation to this rule occurs in narrow and single track lanes where you need to allow *twice* the overall stopping distance that you can see to be clear. This is to allow sufficient room for any oncoming vehicle to brake also.

Overall safe stopping distance

To work out the overall safe stopping distance add thinking distance to braking distance.

Thinking distance + Braking distance = Stopping distance

- **Thinking distance** is the distance travelled in the time between first observing the need for action and acting. The average driver reacts to expected events in 0.7 seconds. The distance covered in that time is the same figure in feet as the speed in miles per hour; for example, at 30 miles per hour thinking distance is 30 feet.

 Actual thinking distance varies according to the speed of the vehicle, your physical and mental condition, your attentiveness and whether or not you are expecting something to happen. Drivers take much longer to react to unexpected events than to expected ones.

- **Braking distance** is the distance needed for braking in dry conditions. You should be familiar with the braking distances for different speeds recommended in the *Highway Code*.

 Actual braking distance depends on the vehicle's capability, the gradient of the road and the condition of the road surface. Rising or falling gradients have a significant effect on deceleration and braking distances. Slippery surfaces greatly increase braking distances.

Do you know your safe stopping distance?

23m, 53m and 96m are the respective shortest stopping distances at 30, 50, and 70 mph.

Do you know what these stopping distances actually look like on the ground? Work out your own pace length (usually less than 1m) and then pace out the three distances. Do this somewhere familiar so that you have a permanent mental image of them.

The two-second rule

One way of keeping a safe distance on fast roads between you and the vehicle in front is by leaving a gap of at least two seconds. But remember your overall stopping distance depends on your speed and the condition of the road surface. An easy way to count two seconds is to say:

Only a fool breaks the two-second rule.

This distance should be at least doubled in wet weather and further increased in icy conditions. If the vehicle behind you is too close, drop back further from the vehicle in front. This will allow you to brake more gently in an emergency and may prevent you being rammed from behind.

Note when the car in front passes a convenient landmark.

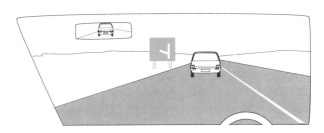

Count one second

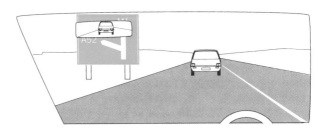

Count two seconds

If you pass the object before you have counted two seconds, you are too close. Drop back and try the test again.

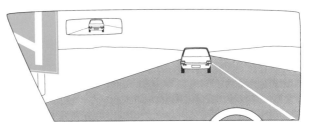

Braking on corners and bends

Because braking affects the balance, stability and cornering ability of vehicles, special care is needed when braking on a corner or bend:

- generally plan to avoid braking on corners because it reduces your ability to steer; if braking is necessary, apply the brakes gently and steadily
- brake in plenty of time
- adjust brake pressure according to the condition or grip of the road surface
- on steep winding descents brake firmly on the straight stretches and gently on the bends; remember to use a low gear at an early stage in the descent.

Do you generally avoid braking when going round corners?

Braking as you approach a hazard

See Chapter 2, The system of car control, page 27

To apply the system of car control you should consider your road speed on the approach to a hazard and adjust it if necessary. If you need to slow down, check your mirrors, adopt the best road position and then reduce speed safely and smoothly using deceleration, braking or a combination of both. Do not forget to check your mirrors before reducing speed or altering direction.

When and how firmly you apply the brakes depends on your judgement of speed and distance. You should consider:

- your initial speed
- the road surface
- weather conditions
- the specific road and traffic conditions.

Sometimes braking may need to be firm but it should never be harsh. Harsh braking usually indicates poor observation, anticipation and planning. Aim to lose speed *steadily* from the first moment until you achieve the right speed to negotiate the hazard. Timing is crucial: avoid braking so early that you have to re-accelerate to reach the hazard, or so late that you have to brake forcefully.

Emergency braking on a good dry road

The quickest and shortest way to stop on a good dry road is to brake to a point just before the wheels lock (technically, the point at which there is 15% wheel slip). In vehicles not fitted with an antilock braking system, many drivers find this degree of finesse in braking difficult to achieve and brake so as to lock their wheels. This also achieves a high degree of braking.

Once the wheels are locked all steering effect is lost. The driver must quickly decide either to brake to a standstill on a straight course if there is enough room or to relax brake pressure to steer out of trouble. One option is to use the cadence braking technique described below. It must be emphasised that antilock braking systems and cadence braking do not assist braking, they assist steering while braking.

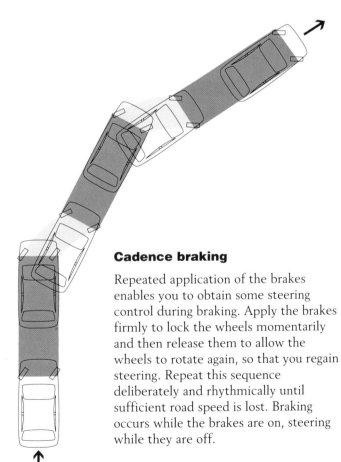

brakes on

brakes off

Cadence braking

Repeated application of the brakes enables you to obtain some steering control during braking. Apply the brakes firmly to lock the wheels momentarily and then release them to allow the wheels to rotate again, so that you regain steering. Repeat this sequence deliberately and rhythmically until sufficient road speed is lost. Braking occurs while the brakes are on, steering while they are off.

Emergency braking on a slippery road

Cadence braking gives you some steering control when braking on a slippery road. However it is much better not to have to brake sharply in these conditions. By careful observation and anticipation you should recognise the likelihood of slippery conditions, and adjust your speed appropriately.

See also Chapter 5, Skidding.

Using the handbrake

Only use the handbrake when the vehicle is stationary. Protect the locking mechanism by pressing the release button whenever you apply or release the handbrake.

Inexperienced drivers are often taught to use the handbrake every time they come to a standstill on a journey. With experience you can judge whether it is necessary to put the handbrake on for every momentary stop.

Steering

A well-maintained vehicle travelling along a flat, straight road should hold its course with minimal steering. Camber, crossfall, or side winds can move the vehicle to one side but a small steering adjustment will compensate for this and keep the vehicle on a straight course. Usually you only need to make positive steering adjustments when you alter course or turn the vehicle.

Steering characteristics vary between vehicles, so make sure you are familiar with the characteristics of vehicles you drive. Some vehicles respond more than average to steering (oversteer) and others less (understeer). Power assisted steering (PAS) assists steering at slow speeds, and may cause those unfamiliar with it to oversteer.

Steering technique

Police driving schools have developed a range of steering techniques to suit different policing situations. The technique most widely adopted by police forces is the pull–push method. This method is generally preferred because it provides safe and efficient steering in a wide range of circumstances. Pull–push and other steering techniques which your instructor may advise you to use are explained on page 74. Other aspects of steering are dealt with more fully in Chapter 8, Cornering.

The steering method you adopt should be determined by the control, efficiency and comfort you experience throughout the full range of steering movements. This may vary according to the car you are driving (the lightness of its steering, the diameter of the steering wheel, the castor action and the number of turns from lock to lock), the position you sit in relation to the steering wheel and your own physiological make up.

Seat position

Good steering starts with getting your body in the right position in relation to the steering wheel. Adjust the position and angle of your seat so that you can reach the controls comfortably. You should aim for a position which allows greatest control of the steering without being uncomfortable. An uncomfortable position causes fatigue and detracts from your driving.

How to hold the steering wheel

- Place your hands on the wheel with your palms on the rim at about the quarter-to-three or ten-to-two position.
- Hold the wheel lightly but be ready to tighten your grip if necessary.
- Keep both hands on the wheel while you are driving unless it is necessary to give an arm signal or to operate a control. Always keep at least one hand on the wheel.

This hold enables you to turn the wheel immediately in either direction. It is common to the majority of safe and efficient steering techniques. It is referred to in this book as the standard hold.

Make changes in direction smoothly and gradually. Make small changes in direction by turning the steering wheel without altering your hand hold.

To make more positive turns, use the pull–push method described on the next page.

Pull–push

With the pull–push method neither hand passes the twelve o'clock position. Your hands remain parallel to each other on the steering wheel except when you move a hand up for the initial pull or when you make small alterations in course. One hand grips and makes the turn, the other slides round its side of the wheel ready to continue the turn. The advantage of pull–push is that it keeps both hands on the wheel and allows an immediate turn in either direction at any point during steering.

The explanation of the pull–push method given below is for a left-hand turn. For a right-hand turn follow the same method but replace left with right, and vice versa.

Start the turn with a pull and not a push because it gives better control.

Slide the left hand up to a higher position on the wheel, but not past the twelve o'clock point.

Pull the wheel down with the left hand.

● As the left hand pulls down, slide the right hand down, allowing the rim to slide through the right hand fingers. Keep the right hand level with the left hand until it nears the bottom of the wheel.

● If more turn to the left is necessary start pushing up with the right hand and at the same time slide the left hand up the wheel, keeping it level with the right.

● Repeat these movements until sufficient turn is obtained.

● Straighten the vehicle after the turn by feeding the wheel back through the hands with similar but opposite movements to those used for the turn. Do not let the wheel spin back on its own.

In certain circumstances, for example during skidding or during very slow or high speed manoeuvres, it may be advantageous to use a different technique from pull–push.

Rotational steering

Hold the wheel using the standard hold described on page 73. The quarter-to-three position allows the greatest degree of turn without having to reposition a hand.

Most alterations to course (up to about 120 degrees of steering wheel turn) can be made by turning the wheel while keeping a light but fixed hand hold.

For more acute bends (requiring more than about 120 degrees of steering wheel turn) reposition your lower hand at 12 o'clock and continue smoothly pulling down the wheel.

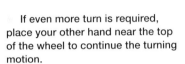

When you can see that a bend is going to require more than 120 degrees of steering wheel turn, place your leading hand at the top of the wheel before starting the turn.

If even more turn is required, place your other hand near the top of the wheel to continue the turning motion.

Straighten the wheel by using a similar series of movements but in the opposite direction. Although the self-centring action of the wheel assists the return, you must keep it under control.

When you steer do you start with a pull rather than a push? If in the past you have tended to start with a push, practise pulling first. Notice how it contributes to the smoothness and control of your steering.

Manoeuvring at slow speeds and in confined spaces

Manoeuvring in a confined space sometimes requires rapid movements of the steering wheel. Generally the standard pull–push technique provides effective steering, but on occasions, especially when reversing, other hand holds may give better control.

Avoid the temptation to turn the steering wheel while the vehicle is stationary. It damages the tyres and puts excessive strain on the steering linkages, particularly in vehicles with power assisted steering. Only turn the steering wheel when the vehicle is moving, even if it is only moving very slowly.

Reversing hold

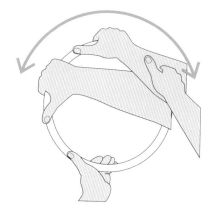

Put one hand at the top of the steering wheel and use this hand to move the wheel. Use the other hand to hold the wheel low down, either loosely while the wheel slides through or tightly when you take a new grip at the top. Look in your mirrors and over your shoulders to get a clear view. You can improve your view to the left by putting your left arm on the back of the seat. If the seat belt restricts your movement, release it but do not forget to put it back on.

Advice on reversing

Reversing can be difficult, especially in a confined area. The faster it is done the more difficult it is to control, so always reverse slowly. Before you reverse:

- scan the area for suitability and obstructions
- ensure you have an unobstructed view
- use mirrors to advantage whilst reversing but do not be totally reliant on them
- wind down your door window to give you more all round awareness
- get someone to help you if possible.

While reversing:

- travel slowly and slip the clutch if necessary – in automatic vehicles you can check the speed by using the left foot on the brake

- remember that, as you steer, the front of your vehicle moves out and could strike nearby objects

- look all round you to make sure there are no hazards.

If your reversing lights fail use your indicator lights or brake-lights to light the area behind you when it is dark, but be careful not to mislead other road users.

Steering guidelines

These are the key points to remember for effective steering:

- do not place your elbows on the window frame or arm rests because this reduces control

- place your hands on the wheel in the ten-to-two or quarter-to-three position: only grip tightly when you need to exert maximum effort

- keep both hands on the wheel when cornering, braking firmly or driving through deep surface water

- on slippery roads steer as delicately as possible or you may skid.

Good steering requires good observation, anticipation and planning. If the brakes are applied sharply or if the speed is too high, steering cannot be precise.

Review

In this chapter we have looked at:

improving your skill in using the basic controls for moving and stopping a vehicle

how to get the maximum safety out of the tyre grip available on your vehicle

how acceleration and braking affect vehicle balance

why it is important to match engine speed to road speed when you change gear

how to use the gears in different circumstances

testing your brakes

why stopping distance is so important, and how to assess safe braking distances

how to use your steering to give you the greatest safety and control.

Check your understanding

How and why does acceleration affect your ability to steer?

How and why does braking affect your ability to steer?

Why do you need to be in the right gear to accelerate?

What is the basic driving safety rule?

When, if at all, should you use your gears to brake?

What is the safest way to lose speed gently in slippery conditions?

How do you calculate overall stopping distance?

What are the factors that affect thinking distance and braking distance?

What are the key points to remember for effective steering?

If you have difficulty in answering any of these questions, look back over the relevant part of this chapter to refresh your memory.

Use this chapter
to find out:

how to minimise
the risk of skidding

what causes a skid

what happens to a
vehicle in a rear
wheel, front wheel
and four wheel
skid

how to correct a
skid.

Chapter 5

Skidding

Developing skill in avoiding and dealing with skids

Driving safely within the limits of the road conditions so that you are able to avoid a skid is better than having to correct one. But however skilful you are, faced with a developing skid you need to know exactly what to do to regain control as quickly as possible, and how to avoid making the skid worse.

This chapter explains the principles and techniques for correcting a skid, but bear in mind that each skid is unique and each vehicle responds differently to skids. How you apply the principles and techniques will depend entirely on the circumstances and on the vehicle you are driving. The best way to gain confidence in dealing with a skid is through formal skidding instruction and there is more information about this at the end of the chapter.

> Because skidding should never be practised on a public road there are no suggestions for practising techniques in this chapter.

Recent developments in vehicle design

Manufacturers are constantly seeking to improve vehicle safety. Antilock braking systems and traction control systems are safety devices that can help safety during braking. Vehicles fitted with these features behave differently from vehicles without, and require you to use different techniques to get the maximum use from them.

Antilock braking systems (ABS)

An increasing number of modern vehicles are fitted with an automatic antilock braking system (ABS). The purpose of an antilock braking system is to retain steering potential during harsh or emergency braking.

ABS can sense the speed at which each wheel is rotating and compare this with pre-programmed data. The system is designed to sense the slowing down of the wheels and to release them before they lock up fully. It reapplies the brakes once the wheels start to rotate again. Once ABS is activated, the driver has to maintain maximum pressure on the brake pedal throughout.

This means that in principle the wheels should never lock, but on a slippery surface the wheels may not rotate immediately the braking pressure is released, allowing momentary lock-up.

ABS does no more than provide the driver with an additional safety device. It does not increase the grip of the tyres on the road, nor can it prevent skidding. In limited circumstances a vehicle equipped with ABS can stop within a shorter distance than if the wheels were locked, but it does not reduce, and could increase, the stopping distance on a slippery surface. If you activate the antilock braking system, this suggests that you are not driving within safe limits.

Traction control systems

Traction control improves steering and vehicle stability by controlling excess wheel slip on individual wheels. It also reduces engine power when there is excessive wheel slip, allowing the wheels to regain traction (or grip) and stability. It allows the vehicle to make maximum use of tyre grip, especially on slippery surfaces and where the friction of the road surface is uneven (for example, where one wheel is on a normal surface and the other on ice or snow).

The technique of skid control is fundamentally different in a vehicle fitted with traction control. Different manufacturers use different systems of traction control, so **if your vehicle has traction control you must consult your vehicle handbook and follow the manufacturer's advice on what to do in skid situations.**

Avoiding skidding

What causes a skid? Many people when asked this question would say that it was the result of poor road or weather conditions, but this is not really true. A skid does not just happen – it is almost always the result of a driver's actions. It is often caused by altering course or speed too harshly for the road conditions.

You should aim to drive and control a vehicle in such a way that it does not skid. This becomes more difficult when road or weather conditions deteriorate, but by using your skills of observation, anticipation and planning you can do a lot to minimise the risks of skidding.

First you need to understand how a skid happens, what warning signs to look out for and what actions to avoid.

How does a skid happen?

A vehicle skids when one or more of the tyres loses normal grip on the road, causing an involuntary movement of the vehicle. This happens when the grip of tyres on the road becomes less than the force or forces acting on the vehicle. The following illustrations explain what these forces are.

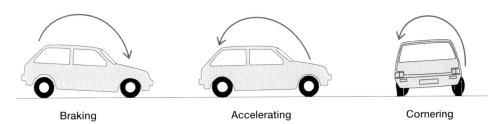

| Braking | Accelerating | Cornering |

These forces act on a vehicle whenever you operate the controls – the brake, the accelerator, the clutch or the steering wheel. If you brake or accelerate while steering round a bend or corner, two forces are combined. As we saw in Chapter 4, there is only limited tyre grip available and if these forces become too powerful they break the grip of the tyres on the road. You should never drive to the limits of the tyre grip available – always leave a safety margin to allow for the unforeseen.

Skidding is usually the result of driving too fast for the conditions. This creates the circumstances from which a skid can develop. If a driver suddenly or forcibly accelerates, brakes, releases the clutch without matching engine speed to road speed or changes direction, this may cause wheel spin. On a slippery road surface, it takes much less force to break the grip of the tyres.

If you have ever experienced a skid, you will probably remember that you were changing either the speed or direction of the vehicle – or both – just before the skid developed.

Causes of skidding

The commonest causes of skidding are:

- excessive speed for the circumstances
- coarse steering in relation to a speed which is not itself excessive
- harsh acceleration
- sudden or excessive braking.

When a skid develops, the driver's first action should be to remove the cause. Later in this section we shall discuss the causes of skidding and how to remove them in more detail.

If you start to skid – remove the cause.

Minimising the risks of skidding

A clear understanding of the causes of skidding should help you to plan to avoid skidding in the first place. In Chapter 3 we talked about the importance of observation, anticipation and planning as the skills which are essential to safe driving and smooth progress. How can you apply these skills to reduce the risks of skidding?

Observe – weather and road conditions to watch for

Skidding is more likely in bad weather conditions and on slippery road surfaces. These are some of the obvious and less obvious hazards you need to watch out for:

- snow, ice, frost, heavy rain
- wet mud, damp leaves or oil, which can create sudden slippery patches on the road surface
- cold spots in shaded areas, under trees, on slopes or hills – watch how other vehicles behave in icy weather

- dry loose dust or gravel
- a shower or rain after a long dry spell – accumulated rubber dust and oil mixed with water can create a very slippery surface
- worn road surfaces that have become polished smooth
- concrete, which usually provides good grip, but which may hold surface water and become slippery in freezing weather
- cobbled roads, still found in some towns and cities, which become very slippery when wet
- changes in the road surface on bridges, which may be more slippery than the surrounding roads.

The risks of these hazards are accentuated at corners and junctions because you are more likely to combine braking, accelerating and steering in these situations.

Anticipate and plan – adjust your driving to the road conditions

Good road observation will enable you to evaluate poor weather and road conditions accurately and adjust your speed accordingly:

- leave plenty of room for manoeuvre, reduce your speed and increase the distance you allow for stopping to match the road conditions – on a slippery surface a vehicle can take many times the normal distance to stop
- use a higher gear in slippery conditions to avoid wheel spin, especially when moving off or travelling at low speeds
- on a slippery surface aim to brake, steer and change gear as smoothly as possible, so that the grip of the tyres is not broken.

Care of the vehicle

Most skids are the result of how a vehicle is driven, but keeping your vehicle in good condition helps to minimise the risk of skidding:

- tyres should be correctly inflated and have adequate tread depth – check tyre treads and tyre pressure regularly
- defective brakes and faulty suspension are especially dangerous on slippery surfaces and may help to cause or aggravate a skid – do not increase the risk by neglecting these problems.

Recognising and removing the cause of a skid

If your vehicle develops a skid you are unlikely to have much time or space in which to correct it. You need to be able to recognise different types of skid in the early stages in order to respond quickly and regain grip between the tyres and the road. When a skid develops, the first action should be to remove the cause.

Cause	How to remove the cause

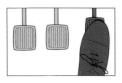

speed or acceleration which is excessive for the road surface

Many skids are caused in this way. At higher speeds you need more tyre grip to corner or stop. When surface grip is low, altering speed or direction can exceed the available grip, causing a skid. The faster you go the more likely this becomes. Harsh acceleration can also cause the wheels to spin, even at low speeds.

One method is to remove pressure from the accelerator and steer to correct the direction of the car. In most cases releasing the accelerator will be sufficient to prevent the skid developing further.

Another method is to depress the clutch to remove the drive from the road wheels, and to steer to correct the direction of the car (see diagrams on pages 86–88). Release the accelerator and keep the clutch pedal depressed until it is safe to re-engage the drive. Re-engage the drive smoothly because any sudden jerkiness can return the car to a skid. Use the accelerator to exactly match the engine speed to the road speed and release the clutch very smoothly.

Do not declutch in vehicles fitted with traction control because it does not operate when the clutch is depressed.

Cause   **How to remove the cause**

excessive or sudden braking

Some skids are caused by braking too harshly for the road conditions – often because of a sudden hazard such as a child running into the road. Excessive braking causes a skid because the tyres lose their grip and the wheels lock up.

Most people's instinctive reaction to a sudden hazard is to brake hard. If a skid then develops the usual response is to want to brake even harder. Learning to overcome this reaction in vehicles not fitted with ABS is crucial.

Relaxing pressure on the brake allows the wheels to rotate, restoring tyre to road surface grip and some directional control. (Do not do this in vehicles fitted with ABS but keep the brakes applied and steer.)

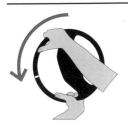

coarse steering

Steering too sharply for the speed of the vehicle increases one of the forces that can break the grip of the tyres on the road. A moving vehicle uses least tyre grip when travelling in a straight line. As soon as you start to corner you place extra demands on the tyre grip. If you steer too sharply for the speed you will break the tyre grip and go into a skid. You can go round the same bend, at the same speed, in the same conditions and lose control by steering harshly instead of smoothly. You should aim to make your steering as smooth as possible.

Reduce speed immediately by either removing pressure on the accelerator or declutching. (Do not declutch in a vehicle fitted with traction control.) This allows the tyres to regain grip on the road, thereby restoring directional control. Steer in the direction you wish to go.

Correcting different types of skid

The action you take to correct a skid depends on what type of skid it is. The illustrations on the following pages show how to recognise and correct a rear wheel, front wheel and four wheel skid. When steering to correct the direction of a car during skidding it may be necessary to use a different technique to pull–push, i.e. rotational steering described on page 75.

Correcting a rear wheel skid

In a rear wheel skid you feel the back of the vehicle swing out – on a corner or bend the swing is always to the outside of the curve. In many situations, removing the cause will quickly correct the skid without having to alter the steering. But if the speed of the vehicle is excessive there may not be sufficient space to regain directional control whatever you do.

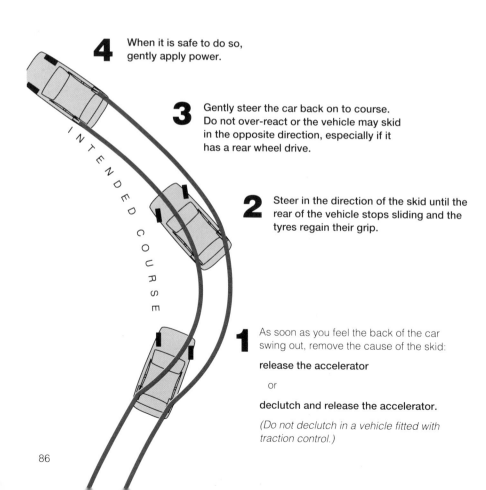

4 When it is safe to do so, gently apply power.

3 Gently steer the car back on to course. Do not over-react or the vehicle may skid in the opposite direction, especially if it has a rear wheel drive.

2 Steer in the direction of the skid until the rear of the vehicle stops sliding and the tyres regain their grip.

1 As soon as you feel the back of the car swing out, remove the cause of the skid:

release the accelerator

or

declutch and release the accelerator.

(Do not declutch in a vehicle fitted with traction control.)

INTENDED COURSE

Correcting a front wheel skid

In a front wheel skid you feel the front of the vehicle carry straight on when you are expecting it to steer left or right. In many situations, removing the cause will quickly correct the skid without having to alter the steering. But if the speed of the vehicle is excessive there may not be sufficient space to regain directional control whatever you do.

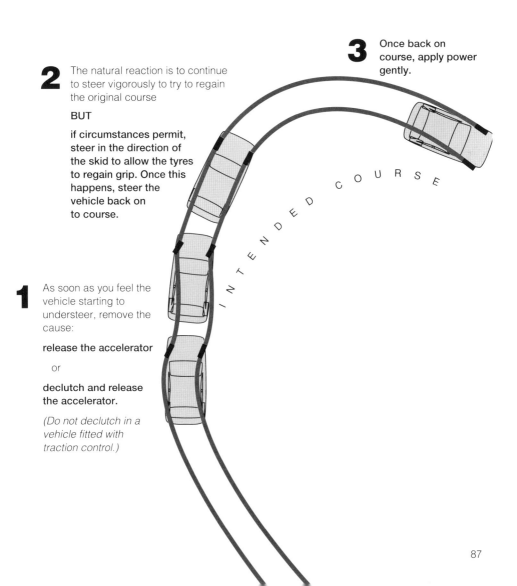

3 Once back on course, apply power gently.

2 The natural reaction is to continue to steer vigorously to try to regain the original course

BUT

if circumstances permit, steer in the direction of the skid to allow the tyres to regain grip. Once this happens, steer the vehicle back on to course.

INTENDED COURSE

1 As soon as you feel the vehicle starting to understeer, remove the cause:

release the accelerator

or

declutch and release the accelerator.

(Do not declutch in a vehicle fitted with traction control.)

Correcting a four wheel skid

In a four wheel skid – usually the result of excessive or sudden braking causing all four wheels to lose grip on the road – you feel a lightness and loss of direction as all four wheels lock up and the vehicle begins to slide. This is most likely where the driver has had to lose speed rapidly in an emergency. Excessive speed is often a contributory cause.

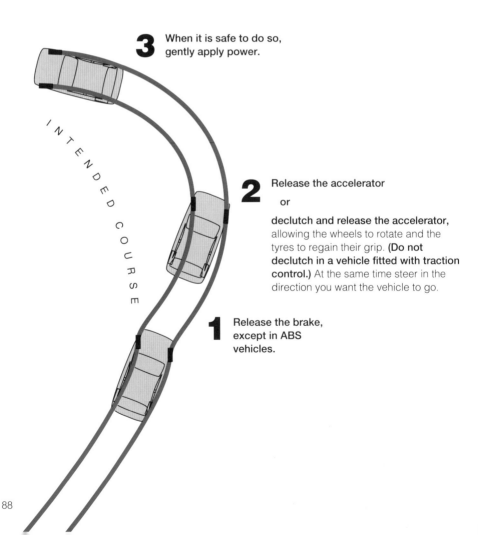

3 When it is safe to do so, gently apply power.

2 Release the accelerator

or

declutch and release the accelerator, allowing the wheels to rotate and the tyres to regain their grip. **(Do not declutch in a vehicle fitted with traction control.)** At the same time steer in the direction you want the vehicle to go.

1 Release the brake, except in ABS vehicles.

Other factors to consider

Once you have removed the initial cause of the skid, your next action may depend on the exact circumstances. For instance:

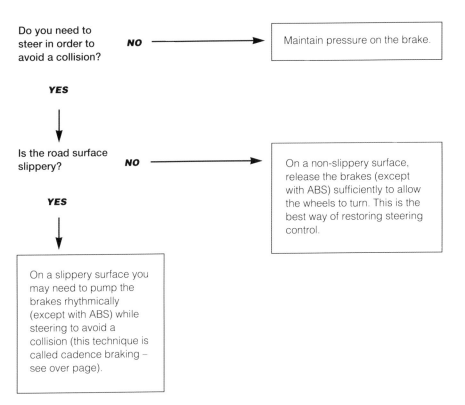

Do you need to steer in order to avoid a collision? **NO** ⟶ Maintain pressure on the brake.

YES

Is the road surface slippery? **NO** ⟶ On a non-slippery surface, release the brakes (except with ABS) sufficiently to allow the wheels to turn. This is the best way of restoring steering control.

YES

On a slippery surface you may need to pump the brakes rhythmically (except with ABS) while steering to avoid a collision (this technique is called cadence braking – see over page).

Vehicles with different drives

Front, rear and four wheel drive vehicles each behave and respond differently when a skid develops. Broadly, the method for correcting a skid is the same for each type of vehicle, but understanding the characteristics of different types of drive can help you anticipate and respond to the vehicle's behaviour more effectively. Refer to your manufacturer's handbook for guidance.

Do you know what type of drive your vehicle has? Get into the habit of mentally noting the type of drive whenever you get into a different vehicle.

Cadence braking
(rhythm braking, pumping the brakes)

The following discussion is only applicable to vehicles not fitted with ABS.

If you brake hard in wet or slippery conditions it is likely that your road wheels will lock and you will lose directional control. Your vehicle will skid in a straight line and you may well collide with something before the skid ends.

See Chapter 4, page 71,
Cadence braking.

If it is necessary to alter course to avoid a collision, you can only regain steering control by allowing the wheels to rotate. Vehicles fitted with ABS do this automatically, but in non-ABS vehicles the greatest degree of control is gained by pumping the brakes rhythmically. Brakes are most effective when they are on the point of locking up, so each time the brake is pumped hard, maximum braking effect takes place. When the brakes are released the wheels rotate and steering control is regained. Cadence braking therefore gives you a combination of braking and steering effect – braking while the brakes are on, steering while they are off.

Pump the brakes with a deliberate movement, pausing momentarily at the full extent of brake pedal travel – avoid bouncing the foot on and off the pedal.

Aquaplaning

Build-up of standing water on the road surface resulting in aquaplaning

One of the most frightening experiences a driver can encounter is aquaplaning. This is where a wedge of water builds up between the front tyres and the road surface, often because of an inadequate depth of tyre tread. Whether you brake or steer, the vehicle will not respond. The safest solution is to remove pressure from the accelerator or to declutch, allowing the vehicle to lose speed and the tyres to regain their grip. Do not turn the steering wheel while aquaplaning because the vehicle will lurch whichever way the wheels are pointing when the tyres regain grip.

Analyse your own experience of skidding

Now that you have a fuller understanding of what causes a skid and how to correct it, think back over your driving career and recall any skids you have had. For each skid you can remember ask yourself:

What were the causes of the skid?

What type of skid was it?

Could you have anticipated these conditions and avoided the skid altogether?

Did you manage to quickly regain directional control? If not, how could you have improved your handling of the skid?

How have you changed your driving as a result of the experience? Has reading this chapter made you aware of further changes that you need to make?

Training in skid correction

Skid correction training can help to:

  raise your standard of driving

  give you confidence in driving under any conditions

  equip you to meet any emergency which might arise.

There are organisations which provide instruction on skidding for members of the public. It is usually given on a skid pan or in a specially designed skid car which can simulate different loss of control situations. Contact your local Road Safety Officer (in the phone book under the name of your local council) who can tell you if instruction is available in your area.

Remember that skidding must never be practised on a public road.

Review

In this chapter we have looked at:

the forces on a vehicle which can break the grip of the tyres on the road

how a driver's actions can cause a skid

reducing the risks of skidding by observing, anticipating, and planning – and by maintaining your vehicle in a good condition

how to recognise and remove the cause of a skid

what a front wheel, rear wheel or four wheel skid feels like and how to correct each type

variations in the characteristics of vehicles with different types of drive

using the technique of pumping the brakes to gain directional control

antilock braking systems and how they work

how to deal with aquaplaning

how to find out about practical skidding instruction.

Check your understanding

What are the causes of skidding?

If a skid is caused by excessive speed, how do you remove the cause?

How would you recognise and correct

• a rear wheel skid?

• a front wheel skid?

• a four wheel skid?

What is 'cadence braking' and when would you use this technique?

What is aquaplaning? What is the safest way to deal with this type of skid?

If you have difficulty in answering any of these questions, look back over the relevant part of this chapter to refresh your memory.

Chapter 6

Driver's signals

*See Chapter 2, The
system of car control,
page 26, Information.*

Developing your skill at using signals

Using signals may seem to be a basic skill, but many drivers do
not use their signals consistently, and do not know how to make
the most effective use of the full range of signals available to
them. This chapter will help you to identify areas in which your
skill at using signals can be developed and improved.

Skill in using signals is an important element in applying the
system of car control. Signalling is one of the key ways in which
we give information to other road users, and giving information
is a key part of the information phase of the system.

The purpose of signals

The purpose of signals is to inform other road users of your
presence or intentions. You should give a signal whenever it
could benefit other road users, but do not signal
indiscriminately.

Only give a signal when another road user will benefit from it.

Signals are used to give information, so they must be given
clearly, in good time and in accordance with the methods
illustrated in the *Highway Code*. As with any communication,
signals can easily be misinterpreted. Always make the meaning
of your signals clear. Other road users use your position and
speed to interpret what your signals mean, so be aware of this,
especially when safety or other considerations cause you to take
an unusual position. These are the key points to remember:

consider the need to give a signal on the approach to every
hazard, and before you change direction or speed

give a signal whenever it could benefit other road users

- remember that signalling does not give you any special right to carry out the actions you indicate
- follow the *Highway Code* – check your mirrors before you signal or manoeuvre.

Avoid confusion

As well as taking care that your own signals are not misleading, you also need to be cautious about how you interpret the signals of other road users. For example, does a vehicle flashing the left-hand indicator mean that the driver intends to:

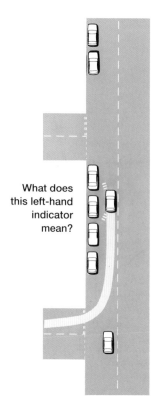

What does this left-hand indicator mean?

- park the vehicle, possibly immediately after a left-hand junction?
- turn into a left-hand junction?
- carry straight on, having forgotten to cancel the last signal?

In practice you should use the position and speed of the vehicle to interpret what the driver intends.

Do you trust the signals of other road users or do you wait for some other confirmation of their intentions?

The range of signals

The signals available to you are:

- indicators
- horn signals
- hazard warning lights
- brakelights
- headlights
- arm signals
- courtesy signals (for example, raising a hand to thank another driver).

On the following pages we look at how you can make best use of these signals, each of which has its advantages and disadvantages. Where there is a choice, consider which signal is likely to be the most effective.

Using the indicators

The system of car control advises you to give a signal only when pedestrians or other road users could benefit. This helps your driving because:

- it encourages you to be attentive and aware of what is happening on the road around you, especially behind you
- it reduces the number of hand movements you have to make
- it reduces signalling clutter; there is always the possibility that your signal could be misinterpreted.

If you decide signalling is appropriate you should give a signal for each manoeuvre you intend to carry out. One signal should not cover two manoeuvres. Use your indicators in accordance with the *Highway Code*, but bear in mind the following points.

- A signal to indicate that you are going to turn left and a signal to indicate that you intend to pull into the side of the road and stop can easily be confused by other road users. If there is a possibility of causing confusion, take steps to avoid it. Consider giving an arm signal to clarify your intentions. Be particularly careful if you intend to park just past a left-hand junction, especially if a vehicle is waiting to emerge.
- Use your position to make your intentions clear to other road users. If you cannot use your road position, or if you think it necessary, reinforce your indicator signal with an arm signal. For example, you indicate to turn right but a parked vehicle causes you to move to the centre of the road just before the junction. Other drivers may think you have indicated to warn of your intention to move out to pass the parked vehicle. Adding an arm signal makes it clear that you intend to turn right.

Cancelling indicator signals

Leaving an indicator working after a turn has been completed confuses other drivers and can easily cause an accident. Do not accept an indicator signal as complete proof of another driver's intention when you are waiting to emerge from a side turning. Look for supporting evidence such as an obvious slowing down before you move out.

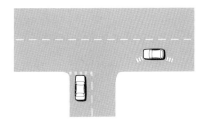

Sometimes the self-cancelling mechanisms do not work, especially when a turn is followed by a bend in the same direction. Take care to cancel the indicator yourself in such situations.

Over the next week monitor how you use indicator signals.

Do you only use them when someone else could benefit?

Do you always use them clearly?

Do you ever back them up with an arm signal?

Do you take care to cancel them promptly?

Identify areas where your use of indicator signals could be improved. Work out what changes you need to make, and decide how and when you will apply them.

Using the horn

Sound your horn when it could benefit pedestrians and other road users in situations where they may not have noticed you or cannot see you.

You should consider using the horn on the approach to any hazard. When you decide it is necessary to sound the horn, alter your position or speed so that you can stop if there is no reaction to your warning. Do not use the horn to challenge or rebuke other road users. Be aware that some people, especially children, the elderly and those with a hearing disability may not hear a horn.

These are the key points to remember:

- first alter your position to avoid the hazard and consider reducing your speed, then sound the horn to inform the other road user(s)
- use your horn in good time
- adjust the length of the horn note to the circumstances
- using the horn does not justify using excessive speed for the circumstances (for example, when driving round a blind bend).

How do you use the horn? Do you use it to help other road users or do you use it as a last resort?

Over the next day or two notice how many times you hear the horn used to assist other drivers, and how many times it is used to rebuke them.

These are examples of circumstances where it could be beneficial to use the horn:

to attract the attention of another road user who is obviously vulnerable (pedestrians and cyclists – especially children – are most at risk)

to inform the driver/s in front of your presence before you overtake

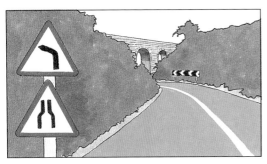

when you approach a hazard where the view is very limited – for example, a blind bend or hump back bridge

to warn the occupants of parked vehicles that you are about to pass them.

Using hazard warning lights

- Only use hazard lights to alert other drivers to your presence when you have stopped. Do not use hazard lights when moving except on unrestricted dual carriageways and motorways. Here you can use hazard lights briefly to warn the vehicles behind that there is a hold-up.

Using brakelights

Brakelights are used to indicate either slowing down or your intention to stop. Remember to check in your mirrors before using your brakes.

- Use your brakelights as an early indication of your intention to slow down. Lightly touch your brakes, well in advance of the anticipated hazard, to alert the driver behind to your intention. This is especially useful when the driver behind is too close.
- Remember that rear foglights are brighter than brakelights and may mask them when you are slowing down.

Flashing your headlights

Use headlight flashes when the horn would not be heard, and in place of the horn at night. Headlight flashes should only be used for one purpose: to inform other road users that you are there. Never assume that a headlight flash from another driver is a signal to proceed. Use a headlight flash in the daylight to:

- alert other drivers to your presence when you are approaching from behind.

Use your judgement to decide the duration of the flash and how far in advance you should give it. This is critical and will depend on your speed. The purpose of the flash is to inform the driver in front of your presence, not that you intend to overtake. It does not give you the right to overtake. Use it when speed makes it likely that the horn would not be heard.

During darkness use headlight flashes to inform other road users of your presence:

- on the approach to a hill crest or narrow hump back bridge
- when travelling along very narrow, winding roads
- before overtaking another vehicle – flash your headlights early enough to enable the driver of the other vehicle to react to them.

Do not give these signals when they might be misunderstood by road users for whom they are not intended.

Using arm signals

Although arm signals are no longer in regular use, you should know what they mean and how to give them in accordance with the *Highway Code*. The general under-use of arm signals makes them stand out, and other road users are more likely to notice them.

Arm signals are especially useful in reinforcing other signals in ambiguous situations. Common situations where they could be useful are:

to reinforce a right-hand turn indicator in an unclear situation

to reinforce brakelights on the approach to a pedestrian crossing.

Do not use arm signals when you need both hands on the steering wheel to control the car, such as during heavy braking at speed or sharp cornering.

Using courtesy signals

Courtesy signals are important because they encourage cooperative use of the road space and promote road safety. Acknowledging the courtesy of other road users encourages good driving and helps you to develop a positive attitude to driving. Using a courtesy signal to apologise or defuse a potential conflict can make a real difference to road safety. Use courtesy signals:

  to thank another driver for letting you go first

  to apologise when you have unintentionally caused inconvenience.

Use either hand to give a courtesy signal but not at the risk of your steering control. You can signal without removing your hand from the wheel by raising your palm or nodding your head. Or you can ask your passenger to signal for you.

On your route home from work, aim to increase the number of courtesy signals that you give and acknowledge (providing it is safe to do so).

How does this affect your state of mind?

Does it influence the actions of other drivers?

If you find you are reluctant to increase the number of courtesy signals you give, ask yourself why. What does this say about your attitudes to your own driving and to other road users?

Responding to other people's signals

Signals other than those given by authorised officials should be treated with caution. If someone beckons you to move forward, always check for yourself whether it is safe to do so.

Review

In this chapter we have looked at:

the place of signals in the system of car control

why it is important to give signals clearly

the different signals available to you, and how and when to use them

how courtesy signals can contribute to road safety.

Check your understanding

When should you consider signalling?

What should you do before you signal or manoeuvre?

Why must you take care in interpreting the signals of other road users?

Why should you only signal when someone else could benefit?

Why do left-hand junctions pose problems for interpreting indicator signals?

In what circumstances should hazard warning lights be used?

What are the guidelines for using the horn?

Explain why you might use arm signals to reinforce other signals.

How do courtesy signals contribute to road safety?

If you have difficulty in answering any of these questions, look back over the relevant part of this chapter to refresh your memory.

See Chapter 2, The system of car control, page 26.

In choosing your road position never sacrifice safety for any other advantage.

Chapter 7

Positioning

Developing skill at positioning your vehicle

Positioning is a crucial element in the system of car control, and this chapter looks at the key factors that you need to consider when deciding how to position your vehicle in different circumstances.

The ideal road position depends on many things: safety, observation, traffic conditions, road layout, cornering, manoeuvrability, assisting traffic flow and making your intentions clear. The overriding consideration is safety, which should never be sacrificed for any other advantage. In so far as there is a standard position on the road, it is the one which gives you the best view but with careful regard to safety.

Zones of different risk

Position is critical to safety. By carefully choosing your position you can do much to reduce the risk of having an accident. Think of the road as zones of different risk. To the nearside there is a risk of coming into conflict with cyclists and pedestrians (especially children), and parked vehicles and their occupants. To the offside, there is a risk of coming into conflict with oncoming vehicles. Between the two extremes there is a relatively safe zone in which to progress. This is towards the left of the centre of the road, giving sufficient clearance to pedestrians and other nearside hazards.

This is only a very general area of safety and you must adapt your position to the actual circumstances.

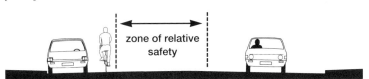

zone of relative safety

Positioning on the approach to hazards

The system of car control provides a safe and methodical approach to hazards. Part of this approach is an awareness of the likely risks involved. This section describes the factors you should take into account as you position your vehicle to approach and pass hazards.

As you approach a hazard you need to be aware that risks can arise from the sides of the road. Dangers can come from anywhere but you will generally have less time to react to hazards coming from the nearside. In narrow roads and one-way systems you need to be equally attentive to both sides of the road.

Roadside hazards

Common roadside hazards that you should be aware of are:

- pedestrians, especially children, stepping off the footpath
- parked vehicles and their occupants
- cyclists, especially children
- concealed junctions.

If you identify hazards on the nearside, steer a course closer to the crown of the road. This has two benefits:

- it gives you a better view
- it provides more space in which to take avoiding action should this become necessary.

If oncoming traffic makes it unsafe to adopt this position or if the road is too narrow, reduce your speed. There is an important trade-off between your speed and the clearance around your vehicle. The less space you have the slower you should go.

The less space you have the slower you should go

When you drive along a row of parked vehicles get into the habit of asking yourself 'Could I stop in time if a child ran out?'

Keep as far from rows of parked vehicles as the circumstances allow. There is always the possibility that a pedestrian, especially a child, might run out from between them, or that an occupant might suddenly step out into your path. If traffic or road conditions prevent you from moving out, slow down. A good rule of thumb is to try to give at least an open door's clearance to the side of any parked vehicles.

One third of children involved in road accidents did not look first.

Improving the view into nearside road junctions

Position yourself so that you can see as much of the road ahead as possible and so that other road users can see you. You can improve your view into nearside roads by positioning your vehicle towards the crown of the road. This also makes you more visible to vehicles pulling out from nearside junctions. You must, however, take into account any vehicles on your offside. Adopt a position that minimises the overall danger from both sides of the road.

Review your skill at positioning for safety

On your next journey, monitor your road positioning from the viewpoint of safety.

Do you pay enough attention to:

- nearside hazards?   ● offside hazards?

Do you position your vehicle to obtain the best view in the circumstances, with due regard to safety?

Are there ways in which you could improve your positioning in order to increase safety?

If traffic conditions allow, a course closer to the crown of the road gives you a better view and provides more space in which to take avoiding action.

Following position

In a stream of traffic, always keep a safe distance behind the vehicle in front. A guide for following distances in open conditions is one metre/yard per mph between you and the vehicle in front. In urban areas, where speeds are lower, a minimum following distance of one foot per mph is advised. (See the section on stopping distances in the *Highway Code*.)

These are some of the advantages of keeping your distance from the vehicle in front:

- you have a good view, and can increase it along both sides by slight changes of position – this enables you to be fully aware of what is happening on the road ahead

- you can stop your vehicle safely if the driver in front brakes firmly without warning

- you can extend your braking distance so that the driver behind has more time to react

- you can see when it is safe to move up into the overtaking position.

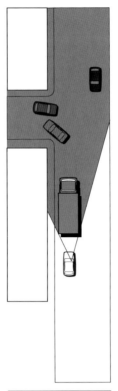

In this illustration the driver is following too closely to the vehicle in front. The aerial plan shows how hazards in the shaded area cannot be seen.

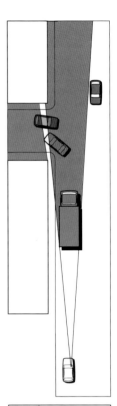

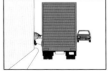

In this illustration the driver is keeping a good safe position and all the hazards are visible. This view could be improved by moving slightly to the nearside or offside.

Over the last month have you had to brake severely to avoid running into a vehicle in front?

If this has happened more than once, were the situations similar?

How have you altered your driving to prevent this happening again?

Overtaking position

When you can see that there are no hazards ahead and you have identified an opportunity to overtake, you should move into the overtaking position. This is closer to the vehicle in front than the following position and you should only use it in readiness for overtaking. If an observed or anticipated hazard comes into view you must move back to a safe following distance from the vehicle in front.

See Chapter 9, Overtaking, page 131. Stage two: the overtaking position.

As you move closer to the vehicle in front the driver is likely to realise that you want to overtake. You must be careful not to intimidate the other driver or to appear aggressive by following too closely. Such misunderstandings are dangerous and counter-productive. They can cause the other driver to speed up, making it more difficult to overtake.

Position for turning

Your position for turning depends on the other traffic, the road layout, the position of any obstacles and the effect of these obstacles on traffic behaviour. Generally the best position on the approach to the junction where you are going to turn is on the nearside of the road for a left turn and towards the centre line for a right turn.

If you intend to turn right and oncoming traffic is encroaching on your side of the road, move away from the centre line.

Give careful consideration to:

| traffic light filter arrows | carriageway markings | other traffic | obstructions. |

If you intend to turn left and the corner has a sharp angle, or is obscured, or pedestrians are present, approach the corner from further out than normal. Avoid 'swan necking', which is approaching close to the nearside and then swinging out to the right just before turning left into the junction.

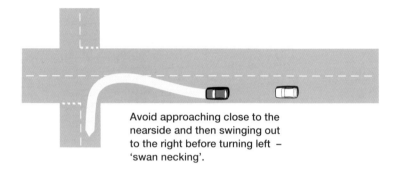

Avoid approaching close to the nearside and then swinging out to the right before turning left – 'swan necking'.

Crossroads

The *Highway Code* advises that two vehicles turning across each other at a crossroads should pass each other offside to offside. But where traffic conditions, the junction layout or local practice makes this impractical, you should pass nearside to nearside. Take extra care on a nearside to nearside pass because your view of the road is obstructed by the other vehicle. Look carefully for oncoming traffic.

Passing
offside to offside

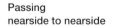

Passing
nearside to nearside

Take extra care on a nearside to nearside pass because your view of the road is obstructed by the other vehicle. Look carefully for oncoming traffic.

Position for stopping behind other vehicles

Before you come to a stop think about your next move. Position your vehicle so that you can continue with minimum inconvenience to yourself and other road users.

When you stop behind a line of vehicles and there is no one following, consider stopping well short of the vehicle in front and watch for traffic coming up behind. If an approaching vehicle appears to have left braking too late, move forward to allow it extra space to stop in. An example of this is where there are traffic lights at a roadworks close to a bend. You should consider stopping in the bend so that the drivers of following vehicles can see you as they approach the bend.

Leave yourself sufficient room to pull out and pass the vehicle in front if necessary.

A good rule of thumb for judging this distance is to stop so that you can see the rear tyres of the vehicle in front.

Parking

Park your vehicle safely: do not leave it where it can cause inconvenience or danger to others. If you park on a hill, put the vehicle in a low gear and consider turning your wheels into the kerb.

Review

In this chapter we have looked at:

the overriding importance of safety in choosing a road position

why a position towards the centre of the road is relatively risk free

common roadside hazards that you need to be aware of

where to position your vehicle if nearside hazards are present

where to position your vehicle while following a vehicle in front

how to position your vehicle for turning and stopping

how to turn past another vehicle at a crossroads.

Check your understanding

What is the overriding factor in determining your road position?

List the common nearside and offside risks that you should take into account when deciding on your position.

If you drive down a road where the space to the sides is restricted, what should you do?

How much clearance should you generally give parked vehicles?

How can you improve your view into nearside junctions?

What are the advantages of keeping your distance from the vehicle in front?

How should you approach a left-hand junction when pedestrians are present?

Why do you need to be careful if you pass nearside to nearside at a junction?

If you have difficulty in answering any of these questions, look back over the relevant part of this chapter to refresh your memory.

See Chapter 2 The system of car control, page 21.

Chapter 8

Cornering

Developing your skill at cornering

'Cornering' means driving a car round a corner, curve or bend. Cornering is one of the main driving activities, and it is important to get it right. When you corner your vehicle loses stability, and you place extra demands on the tyre grip available. The faster you go and the tighter the bend, the greater these demands are.

This chapter explains how to apply the system of car control to cornering. Every bend is different and varies with the traffic and weather, but the first part of the chapter sets out the general principles of cornering that will help you to drive round all corners and bends safely.

The next section explains the forces involved in cornering, and the factors that can increase or reduce your vehicle's ability to corner safely. The final part of the chapter explains in illustrated detail how to use the system of car control in conjunction with limit point analysis. This technique, used together with the system of car control, provides a clear and consistent way of assessing safe cornering speeds.

The system of car control – principles for safe cornering

Cornering is potentially dangerous so you should use the system of car control to help you carry out the manoeuvre safely. Each phase of the system is relevant, but the information phase is especially important. Correctly assessing the severity of the bend is essential for safety. Applying the system and the safe stopping rule gives us four key principles of safe cornering:

- your vehicle should be in the right position on the approach
- you should be travelling at the right speed for the corner or bend
- you should have the right gear for that speed
- you should be able to stop on your own side of the road in the distance you can see to be clear.

Applying these principles to the variations in bend, traffic conditions, road surface conditions, visibility and other factors requires good judgement and planning. But before we look in more detail at using the system of car control for cornering, it is helpful to consider the other key factors that affect a vehicle's ability to corner safely.

> Think back to any occasions when you have experienced a loss of control while cornering. For each occasion work out why this happened and how you could prevent it happening again.
>
> Examine each situation for the influence of the following factors:
>
> ● poor observation
>
> ● poor anticipation
>
> ● poor planning.

Cornering forces

A moving vehicle is at its most stable when travelling in a straight line on a level course and at constant speed. It will continue to travel on a straight course unless you apply some other force to alter its direction. When you steer, the turning force to alter direction comes from the action of the front tyres on the road. We saw in Chapter 4 that this force depends on tyre grip. If the front tyre grip is broken, the car will continue in a straight line. On tighter bends, at higher speeds and in heavier vehicles, the demands on tyre grip are greater.

(As you corner, your body feels as if it is being pushed out towards the side of the car. In fact it is continuing to move in a straight line and only turns into the bend because it is forced to by the car.)

You will recall from Chapter 4 that tyre grip faces competing demands from three forces:

steering

accelerating

braking.

The more you brake or accelerate the less tyre grip you have for steering. The faster you go into a corner or bend, the greater the tyre grip required to keep you on course round it.

The practical outcome of these forces is to cause vehicles to continue in a straight line rather than turning whenever tyre grip is lost. So in a left-hand bend, as tyre grip is lost, your vehicle drifts to the right of your intended course and in a right-hand bend it drifts to the left. The design of the vehicle will reduce or accentuate these tendencies.

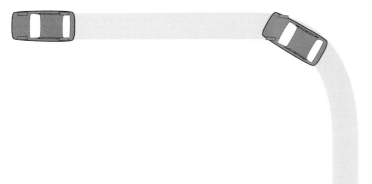

Tendency of a
vehicle to continue
in a straight line

Vehicle characteristics

Roadworthiness

Vehicles vary in their ability to corner, and they only corner to the best of their ability if they are well maintained. Steering, suspension, shock absorbers, tyres, tyre pressures and the loading of the vehicle all affect its balance and road grip when cornering. Make sure that your vehicle and tyres are in good condition and that your tyre pressures are kept at the recommended levels. Also position loads so that they do not upset the balance of the vehicle.

Vehicle specification

The specifications that affect the handling characteristics of a vehicle are:

- the type of drive (front wheel, rear wheel or four wheel)
- suspension and damping
- traction control, if fitted
- adaptive suspension, if fitted
- the drive ratio and central differential characteristics on a four wheel drive vehicle.

Understeer and oversteer

Understeer is the tendency of a vehicle to turn less, and oversteer is the tendency of a vehicle to turn more in response to a given turn of the steering wheel. The tendency to understeer or oversteer is a characteristic of the vehicle itself and depends primarily on what sort of drive the vehicle has. In general, front wheel drive vehicles understeer and rear wheel drive vehicles oversteer. Make a point of knowing whether your vehicle understeers or oversteers and adapt your driving to the characteristics of your vehicle on corners and bends.

Understeer

Oversteer

In a front wheel drive car, you will increase understeer if you:

enter the bend at too high a speed

apply power in the bend

steer too sharply.

You can reduce this understeer by partially reducing power and/or steering. But if power is reduced by too much too suddenly, you may convert the understeer to oversteer.

A rear wheel drive car initially behaves in the same way, but if excessive power is applied on a slippery surface the understeer may convert quite suddenly to oversteer. This requires a prompt steering correction in the opposite direction to the bend.

Four wheel drive cars provide better road adhesion all round but when driven to extremes they will behave in a similar way to the front or rear wheel drive model from which they are derived.

Camber and superelevation

The road surface is not normally level across its width but is built with a slope to assist drainage. The slope across the road affects steering. The normal slope falls from the crown of the road to the edges and is called camber.

On a left-hand bend camber increases the effect of your steering because the road slopes down in the direction of turn.

On a right-hand bend camber reduces the effect of steering because the road slopes away from the direction of turn.

(This only applies if you keep to your own side of the road. If you cross over the crown to the other side of the road, camber will have the opposite effect on steering.)

There are many instances, especially at junctions, where the slope across the road surface is at an unexpected angle. Whatever the slope, if it falls in the direction of your turn it will increase the effect of your steering; if it rises in the direction of your turn it will reduce the effect of your steering. You need to consider the slope across the road when deciding on your speed for a bend.

Superelevation is where the whole width of the road is banked up towards the outside edge of the bend, making the slope favourable for cornering in both directions.

Crown camber

Superelevation

Observe the effects of camber on your steering

Next time you make a short journey, observe the camber every time you corner.

Can you identify three sections of road on any of the routes that you regularly use where the slope across the road surface makes cornering difficult?

Next time you have a safe opportunity on a stretch of straight road where the camber is normal (sloping from the crown to the edge of the road), steer a course towards the left of the centre of the road. Momentarily lighten your grip on the steering wheel and notice the effect of the camber as your vehicle moves to the left. Almost immediately retighten your grip and correct your course. Only do this exercise if it is totally safe, giving due regard to other vehicles and your speed. Use the system of car control to carry it out.

As you go round bends observe the effect of the camber on your cornering and notice its effect on the steering and balance of your vehicle.

Summary of factors affecting cornering

To sum up, the factors that determine your vehicle's ability to corner are:

speed

the amount of steering you apply

the amount of acceleration and/or braking

the characteristics of the vehicle

the slope across the road surface – camber and superelevation

the road surface and how the weather has affected its grip.

The system of car control and the limit point

Now that you can identify the factors which affect your vehicle's ability to corner, the following section explains in detail how to use the system of car control and the limit point to corner safely.

The system of car control assists planning in approaching and negotiating corners and bends. The five phases of the system – information, position, speed, gear and acceleration – highlight the essential factors that you must consider when cornering.

As you approach a bend using the system you should be seeking as much information as possible about the severity of the bend. You should use all the observational aids and clues available to you (weather, road surface, road signs, road markings, the line made by lamp posts and trees, the speed and position of oncoming traffic, the angle of headlights at night, etc) to anticipate and plan for the severity of the bend. A valuable aid to observation is the limit point because it gives you a systematic way of judging the correct speed through the bend.

How to use the limit point to help you corner

The limit point is the furthest point along a road to which you have an uninterrupted view of the road surface. On a level stretch of road this will be where the right-hand side of the road appears to intersect with the left-hand side of the road. This point of intersection is known as the limit point. To drive safely you must be able to stop on your own side of the road within the distance you can see to be clear – that is, the distance between you and the limit point.

The ability to stop on your own side of the road in the distance you can see to be clear determines how fast you can go. The more distant the limit point the faster you can go because you have more space to stop in. The closer the limit point the slower you must go because you have less space to stop in.

Match your speed to the speed at which the limit point moves away from you providing you can stop within the distance that you can see to be clear.

As you approach and go through a bend the limit point appears at first to remain stationary as you approach it, then to move away at a constant speed and finally to sprint away to the horizon as you come out of the bend. The technique of limit point analysis is to match your speed to the speed at which the limit point appears to move. If it is moving away from you, accelerate. If it is coming closer to you or standing still, decelerate or brake. Even if the bend is not constant, you can still match your speed to the apparent movement of the limit point, because this will vary with the curvature of the bend.

Approaching the bend

At first the limit point appears to remain at the same point in the road. Reduce your speed to be able to stop safely within the remaining distance.

As you approach the bend take information about the sharpness of the bend and carefully assess the appropriate speed for cornering.

1

2

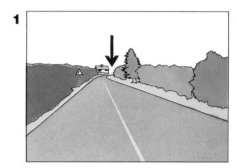

3

Going through the bend

Just before you enter the bend the limit point begins to move round at a constant speed. Adjust your speed to the speed of this movement.

You now have the correct speed for the bend. Select the gear to match this speed before entering the bend.

Coming out of the bend

As the bend starts to straighten out your view begins to extend, and the limit point starts to move away more quickly. You then accelerate towards the limit point in proportion to the straightening out of your steering.

As the bend comes to an end, continue to accelerate to catch the limit point until other considerations such as speed limits or new hazards restrict your acceleration.

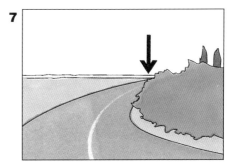

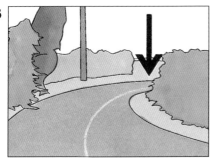

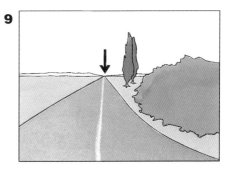

These are the advantages of using the limit point together with the system:

- it ensures that you observe the driving safety rule of matching your speed to your ability to stop within the distance you can see to be clear
- it gives you the appropriate speed to approach and negotiate the bend
- it gives you the appropriate speed to go round the bend, and therefore the appropriate gear to be in
- it gives the point at which to start accelerating
- it is self-adjusting: as road visibility and conditions deteriorate you need more distance in which to stop, and so your speed must be reduced to compensate.

> Over the next two weeks practise matching your road speed to the movement of the limit point. Remember to adjust your speed so that you are able to stop on your own side of the road in the distance you can see to be clear.
>
> Make a special point of using the limit point to set your speed for bends and corners on roads you know well. It is on familiar routes that attention often wanders.

How to use the system for cornering

This section takes you through the five phases of the system identifying key considerations at each phase and explaining how to use limit point analysis in the speed phase. As with any other use of the system, you should work through it methodically selecting the phases that are appropriate.

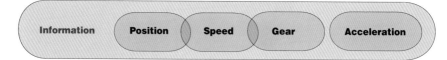

Information · Position · Speed · Gear · Acceleration

Information phase

On the approach to a corner or bend you should be constantly scanning the road for information, but specifically you need to look for:

- the traffic in front and behind
- the road surface and the effect of weather conditions on it
- the limit point.

Seek out opportunities to look across the bend through gaps in hedges or between buildings. Look at the line of curvature of hedgerows and lamp posts to give you more information about the severity of the bend. But avoid becoming preoccupied with the bend – look for early warning of other hazards as well.

Position phase

You need to consider three things when deciding where to position your vehicle for cornering:

- safety
- information needs
- reducing the tightness of the bend.

Safety

Position yourself so that you are least likely to come into conflict with other road users: for example, look out for pedestrians to your nearside and oncoming traffic to your offside. Safety is the overriding consideration. If you can safely adopt one of the positions suggested below do so but never sacrifice safety for position.

Information needs

Your road position will determine how much you can see when you enter a bend. The position which gives you the greatest view depends on whether the bend is a left-hand bend or a right-hand bend.

- **Right-hand bends** – position yourself towards the left of your road space. Be wary of parked vehicles and pedestrians and give them sufficient clearance. Other dangers to consider are blind junctions or exits, adverse cambers and poor condition of the nearside road surface.

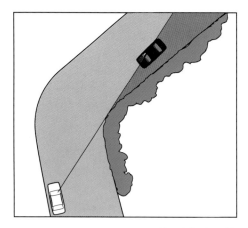
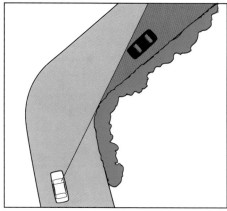

For right-hand bends, the nearside gives an earlier view
into the bend

Left-hand bends – position yourself towards the centre
line so that you get an early view round the bend.
Before you adopt this position consider:

- approaching traffic and other offside dangers which
  require a greater margin of safety

- whether your position might mislead other traffic as to
  your intentions

- whether any advantage would be gained at low speed
  or on an open bend.

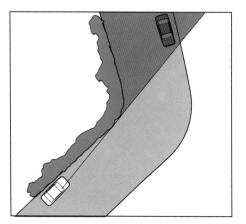
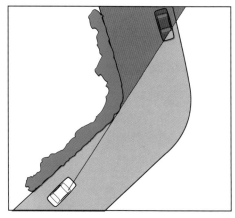

For left-hand bends, a position towards the centre of the road
gives an earlier view

Reducing the tightness of the bend

The other thing to consider is reducing the tightness of the curve through which you drive. By moving your vehicle from one side of the available road space to the other you can follow a shallower curve and thereby improve stability. The path you take is different for a right- or a left-hand bend, but always consider safety first. Do not take a straighter course unless you can see ahead clearly. Often you will not be able to do this until the road begins to straighten out.

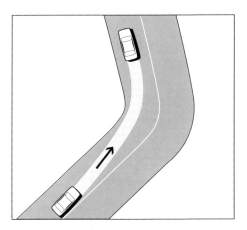

Reducing the curvature of left-hand bends

Keep towards the centre line until you can see clearly ahead. Then drive your vehicle through a gradual curved path towards the nearside of the road, moving into a more normal position on the other side of the bend.

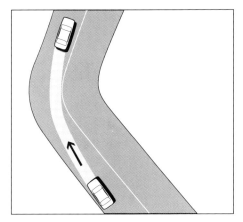

Reducing the curvature of right-hand bends

If you have a view across a bend and there is no oncoming traffic, take a gradually curving path towards the centre of the road. Then ease the vehicle back towards a more normal position on the other side of the bend. Under no circumstances must any other road users be endangered. Look at the diagram to the left and you can see that the curve made by the vehicle following this course is straighter than the curve of the bend itself.

When you are cornering, practise using the available road space to improve your ability to observe, and to reduce the curvature of the bend. Make sure there is no possibility of coming into conflict with other road users.

Do this consistently for three days. Notice how it improves your ability to see, and the smoothness and stability of the drive.

Speed phase

When you have adopted an appropriate position, the next phase of the system is to consider and obtain the appropriate speed to enter the bend.

Use the limit point to judge the safe speed to drive round the bend. Where the curve round the bend is constant, the limit point moves away from you at a constant speed. This gives you the speed for the bend unless the curvature changes. If the bend tightens, the limit point appears to move closer to you, and you should adjust your speed accordingly to remain within the safe stopping distance.

When assessing the speed to go round a bend, you need to consider:

  your vehicle's characteristics

  the road and road surface conditions

  the traffic conditions

  the weather conditions.

When you assess the situation, do not think, 'What is the fastest that I can go round this bend?' but rather, 'Can I stop in the distance I can see to be clear?' – that is, just before the limit point.

Gear phase

When you have achieved the right speed and before entering the bend, engage the appropriate gear for that speed. Select the gear that gives you greatest flexibility.

Think also about your expected acceleration on the far side of the bend. If you expect to come out of the bend into a 30 mph area, then gentle acceleration would be appropriate. If the speed restriction on the other side of the bend is the national speed limit, consider entering the bend in a gear that will provide maximum acceleration out of it. The condition of the road surface needs to be included in these considerations: in wet or slippery conditions, harsh acceleration in a low gear may well result in wheel spin and a loss of steering control.

See Chapter 4,
Acceleration, using
gears, braking and
steering, page 61.
Using the gears.

Acceleration phase

Providing there are no additional hazards, start to accelerate when the limit point begins to move away and you begin to straighten your steering.

As you continue to straighten your steering, increase your acceleration to 'catch' the limit point. Accelerate until you reach the speed limit or other considerations restrict your speed.

Review

In this chapter we have looked at:

the four principles of safe cornering

the forces acting on a vehicle on bends and corners

why vehicles are less stable when cornering

the characteristics that affect a vehicle's ability to corner

how camber affects the ability to corner

the use of the system of car control for cornering

the technique of limit point analysis

how to position yourself on the approach to a bend

how to reduce the curvature of a bend

how to assess the speed for a bend.

Check your understanding

What are the four principles of safe cornering?

Why are vehicles less stable when cornering?

Why are you less able to steer if you brake or accelerate sharply?

In which direction do you go if tyre grip is lost on a right-hand bend?

Why is the fall of the camber an important consideration during cornering?

What is meant by the limit point and how do you use it to corner safely?

Explain where to position your vehicle during cornering, taking account of safety, observation and reducing the curvature of the bend.

If you have difficulty in answering any of these questions, look back over the relevant part of this chapter to refresh your memory.

Chapter 9

Overtaking

Developing your skill at overtaking safely

This chapter explains how to use the system of car control to overtake and identifies the additional hazards that you need to consider to carry out the manoeuvre safely.

Overtaking is hazardous because it may bring you into the path of other vehicles. It is a complex manoeuvre because you need to consider a number of subsidiary hazards as well as the primary hazard presented by the vehicle(s) to be overtaken. Applying the system of car control enables you to carry out the manoeuvre safely.

Key safety points

When considering whether to overtake, always follow this safety advice:

- do not overtake where you cannot see far enough ahead to be sure it is safe

- avoid causing other vehicles (overtaken, following or approaching) to alter course or speed

- always be able to move back to the nearside in plenty of time

- always be ready to abandon overtaking if a new hazard comes into view

- do not overtake in situations where you might come into conflict with other road users (these are identified in the overtaking section of the *Highway Code*)

- avoid making a third line of moving vehicles wherever possible

- never overtake on the nearside on dual carriageways except in slow-moving queues of traffic when offside queues are moving more slowly.

Remember that overtaking is your decision and you can reconsider it at any point.

Overtaking places you in a zone of potential danger, and requires good judgement if it is to be safe. The ability to overtake with consistent safety only comes with experience and practice. Even when you have acquired this skill you need to be extremely cautious. Always be patient and leave a margin of safety to allow for errors. If in doubt hold back.

Practise applying the key safety points

Write out the seven points of the overtaking safety advice listed above. (If you cannot recall the *Highway Code* advice obtain a current edition and refresh your memory.) Take your list with you the next time you drive and monitor how well you follow the advice in the relevant situations. When you get an opportunity for a break, go through the list and mark the points that you failed to consider or comply with fully.

Work out why you did not follow the advice and plan a way of improving your future performance. Note this down and review your performance again in a fortnight.

Overtaking stationary vehicles

Overtaking stationary vehicles is relatively straightforward. Use the system to approach and assess the hazard, and to pass it with safety. Take account of the position and speed of oncoming traffic, the position and speed of following traffic and the presence of pedestrians. If the situation allows, keep at least a door's width away from the side of the stationary vehicle.

Sometimes a slow-moving vehicle such as a heavy lorry climbing uphill can be regarded as a stationary object. As speeds increase, however, planning becomes more difficult and judgement more critical.

Overtaking moving vehicles

Overtaking a moving vehicle is more complicated because the hazards are moving and the situation changes all the time. You need to consider the speed and acceleration capabilities of your own vehicle, and the relative speeds of other vehicles. You also need to be able to predict where vehicles and gaps in the traffic will converge. To do this safely requires careful observation and planning, good judgement of speed and distance, and an awareness of the many possible secondary hazards.

How to overtake

When you are catching up with another vehicle you should decide whether to adjust your speed and follow while it makes reasonable progress, or to overtake at the first safe opportunity. Whatever your decision, careful use of acceleration sense will assist the ease and smoothness of your manoeuvre. If you decide to overtake, assess whether you can approach and overtake in one continuous manoeuvre, or whether you will have to follow for a while until a suitable opportunity arises. Either way, the vehicle in front is a hazard so you need to consider the various phases of the system to deal with it safely.

You will meet other road users besides vehicles, and you need to consider their special needs. Avoid startling horses. Be aware that cyclists, especially children, can be erratic and allow them plenty of room. Give motorcycles good clearance and be aware that if you are too close your slip stream could destabilise them.

The following pages explain how to use the system of car control to tackle the two overtaking situations we have identified:

the absence of other hazards allows you to approach and overtake in one manoeuvre

other hazards require you to take up a following position before you can overtake.

In real life both these situations may of course develop and become complicated by further hazards, but for the moment our main concern is to explain the two different methods as clearly as possible. The additional hazards you need to consider are identified later in the chapter.

Overtaking in the absence of other hazards

You have identified that there is only one hazard present – the vehicle ahead that you are gaining on – and all the other conditions (such as clear view, sufficient space and absence of oncoming traffic) are suitable for immediate overtaking. Take the decision to overtake and work through the appropriate stages of the system to pass the slower vehicle(s) in one smooth manoeuvre.

Acceleration

Adjust your speed to return to the identified gap, and continue with your journey.

Speed

Adjust your speed to complete the manoeuvre within the road space you know to be clear, and before any approaching vehicle could come into conflict with you.

Position

At the appropriate point, take a course to overtake the vehicle ahead.

Information

Observe the road ahead for road signs and markings, layout, approaching vehicles, other hazards, and any obstructed views which could conceal hazards. Identify a safe return gap. Observe the speed and position of any vehicles behind you. Judge the relative speeds of your own vehicle and the vehicle(s) to be overtaken. Plan your overtaking manoeuvre. Consider the need to signal, and signal if appropriate.

Overtaking when other hazards require you to take up a following position

This occurs when the presence of approaching vehicles, obscured views or some other hazard requires you to follow the vehicle(s) ahead before you can overtake safely. Overtaking in this situation requires a three-stage approach as illustrated on the right.

Stage 3
overtaking

Stage 2
the overtaking position

Stage 1
the following position

Stage one: the following position

Where you are gaining on a vehicle in front, and it is not possible to overtake immediately, use the system of car control to reduce your speed to that of the vehicle in front to follow at a safe distance.

Your main task in the following position is to observe and assess the road and traffic conditions for an opportunity to overtake safely. You need to ask yourself the questions below.

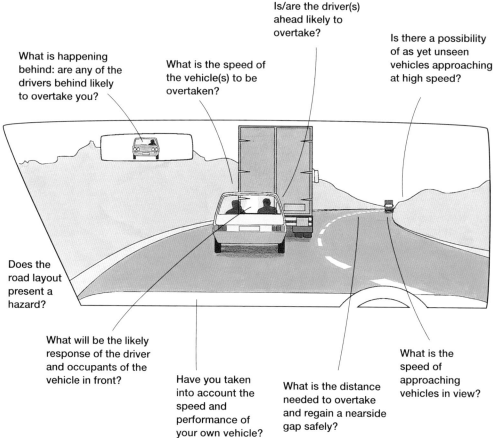

Is/are the driver(s) ahead likely to overtake?

Is there a possibility of as yet unseen vehicles approaching at high speed?

What is happening behind: are any of the drivers behind likely to overtake you?

What is the speed of the vehicle(s) to be overtaken?

Does the road layout present a hazard?

What will be the likely response of the driver and occupants of the vehicle in front?

Have you taken into account the speed and performance of your own vehicle?

What is the distance needed to overtake and regain a nearside gap safely?

What is the speed of approaching vehicles in view?

Observe what is happening in the far distance, the middle ground, the immediate foreground and behind; do this repeatedly and look in the mirror frequently.

Your safety depends on making the correct interpretation of what you see. It is not enough just to see it.

In some circumstances it may be possible, as you close up on a vehicle in front, to miss out stage one and go straight to stage two: the overtaking position. This is determined by your view of the road ahead and whether any additional hazards are present that would make the overtaking position unsafe. If you do go straight to the overtaking position you still need to observe and assess the hazards identified in the diagram.

Stage two: the overtaking position

The overtaking position is closer than the following position and minimises the distance you have to travel to overtake. It can also indicate to the driver in front that you wish to overtake. Adopt this position so that you are ready to overtake when a safe opportunity arises.

Because it is closer than the following position you have less time to react to the actions of the vehicle in front, so you must be sure that there are no hazards ahead which might cause it to brake suddenly. You can only know this if you have been able to fully observe the road ahead.

Work through the stages of the system to move up to the overtaking position.

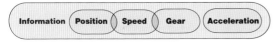

Information

Observe the road ahead and behind for an opportunity to safely occupy the overtaking position. Take into account hazards that can be seen and the possible dangers in areas that cannot be seen. Plan your move when you see an opportunity developing. Consider the need to signal.

Position

Move up to the overtaking position. This is the closest position to the vehicle in front that is consistent with the hazards and that gives an adequate view of the road ahead. It is not possible to define this position exactly, it depends on an awareness of the possible dangers, good judgement and experience. The larger the vehicle in front, the further back you need to be. Also be aware that the closer you get to the vehicle in front the more likely you are to intimidate the driver.

With large vehicles and where it helps, take a view along both sides of the vehicle.

Speed

Adjust your speed to that of the vehicle in front.

Gear

If you are not already in an appropriate gear, select the most responsive gear for the speed, bearing in mind that this is the gear you will use to accelerate as you overtake.

As the overtaking position is closer than the following position you must observe carefully for any new hazards. If a hazard comes into sight consider dropping back to the following position until the hazard is passed. When planning to overtake you need to know exactly what is on the road ahead and to be aware of the possible pitfalls. Observation, planning, judgement of speed and distance and attention to detail are crucial. Thoughtless overtaking is dangerous.

Stage three: overtaking

From the overtaking position continue observing until you identify an opportunity to overtake, then re-run the system of car control to guide you while overtaking.

Information

Identify:

- a safe stretch of road along which you have adequate vision
- a gap into which you can safely return
- the speed of any approaching vehicles
- the relative speed of your own vehicle and the vehicle(s) you intend to overtake
- what is happening behind.

Consider the need to give information: is the driver in front aware of your presence, do you need to signal your intentions to the driver behind? Consider the benefits of giving a headlight, horn or indicator signal.

Position

Having made a thorough information check and decided it is safe to go, recheck your mirrors, give any necessary signals, and move out to an offside position. Generally, do this without accelerating. From this new position make a thorough information check of the road ahead and behind for any unidentified hazards. Decide whether to continue with overtaking.

Speed

Overtake if the situation is clear, adjusting your speed if necessary. While you are in the offside position you are in a zone of potential danger so move through it as briskly as possible.

Gear

Before overtaking you should have adopted a suitable gear for the manoeuvre. Sometimes circumstances may require another gear change, but you should generally avoid changing gear during overtaking itself. Keep both hands on the steering wheel throughout the whole manoeuvre if possible.

Acceleration

Adjust your speed to complete the overtaking manoeuvre safely,

*See Chapter 4,
Acceleration, using gears,
braking and steering,
page 58.*

and to enter the gap you have identified. Use acceleration sense to adjust your speed if possible.

If you are overtaking in a line of traffic and the offside position provides a good view, consider the opportunity for further overtaking before you return to the nearside position. If you have considered all aspects of the system and it is safe to proceed, take the opportunity and move on to the new safe gap that you have identified.

Summary

The diagram below summarises the overtaking manoeuvre described in stage three:

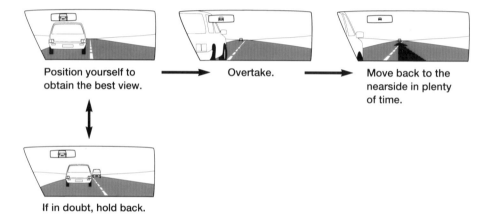

Position yourself to obtain the best view. ➔ Overtake. ➔ Move back to the nearside in plenty of time.

If in doubt, hold back.

Practise the three-stage method of overtaking

Plan a route where there are likely to be hazards that will prevent you from overtaking immediately. Practise the three-stage overtaking method and then review your performance. Ask yourself the following questions:

- Did I have enough information to be sure I was safe at every stage?
- Was my positioning correct at every stage?
- Was I in the right gear at every stage?
- Did I always reach the return gap in good time?
- Was the return gap always big enough?
- Did I miss any overtaking opportunities?

If you had any problems in these areas, work out why. Then work out how to overcome them in future.

Special hazards to consider before attempting to overtake

In the first part of this chapter we have worked through two methods for overtaking systematically. To present these as clearly as possible we have not introduced other aspects of road and traffic conditions which must be considered before overtaking. These considerations are essential to safety, and are explored next.

The *Highway Code* has a section which gives advice on overtaking. The illustrations below show some common accident situations that can arise if this advice is not followed.

The driver of the white car does not realise that the driver of the blue car can see only the slow-moving bus and may move out into the path of the overtaking car

The driver of the white car fails to foresee that the red car may turn without warning into a side road, cutting across the path of the overtaking car

The driver of the white car fails to appreciate that the driver of the green car is looking only to his right and may pull out as the overtaking car approaches on the wrong side of the road

The driver of the white car fails to appreciate that the lorry is not indicating to overtake the car ahead, but is turning right

The range of hazards you must consider

Before overtaking you must consider the full range of possible hazards that each situation presents:

- the vehicle in front
- the vehicles behind
- the road layout and conditions
- road surface
- overtaking in a stream of vehicles
- overtaking on a single carriageway
- right-hand bends
- left-hand bends
- overtaking on a dual carriageway.

Each of these is discussed below.

The vehicle in front

Assess what sort of hazard the vehicle in front presents.

- Has the driver of the vehicle noticed you?
- Can you predict from earlier behaviour whether the response of the driver is likely to be aggressive?
- Does the size or the load of the vehicle prevent the driver from seeing you or prevent you from seeing the road ahead clearly?

Make your intention to overtake clear to the driver in front. Your road position and following distance help you to do this, but take care not to appear too intimidating. This can be counter-productive and provoke an aggressive response in the other driver who might speed up as you try to overtake. If the driver in front appears to be obstructive, consider the implications. Firstly, is it worthwhile overtaking at all and secondly, how much extra speed and space do you need to allow for this?

If the driver in front has not noticed your presence or has loads which obscure the rear view mirrors, take this into account. Consider the use of the headlights or horn to inform the driver of your presence.

Take extra care before overtaking a long vehicle. If appropriate, take views to both sides of the vehicle and ensure that there is ample space to overtake and return safely to your own side. The same applies to vehicles that have wide or high loads: be sure that you have observed carefully and are aware of any possible dangers in the road ahead.

The vehicles behind

Assess whether the vehicles behind pose a risk. Note their speed, position and progress, and judge whether they may attempt to overtake you. Be aware that other vehicles may come forward from behind the vehicle behind you. Consider the need to signal your intentions. Use your mirrors to monitor the situation behind you, especially before changing your speed or position.

Road layout and conditions

When planning to overtake, consider the layout of the road ahead very carefully. Look for nearside obstructions or junctions (including pathways, tracks, entrances, farm gates) out of which vehicles or other hazards could emerge and cause the vehicle(s) you intend to overtake suddenly to veer to the offside. On the offside, look carefully for junctions, especially where they could conceal emerging vehicles or other hazards.

Look for lay-bys on both sides of the road and be alert to the possibility that a vehicle might pull out of them. Be especially attentive to offside lay-bys. Drivers leaving them may not see you because they are concentrating on what is happening behind rather than in front of them.

Bends, hill crests, hump back bridges and any other aspect of road layout which could obscure your view must be taken into account. Allow for the possibility

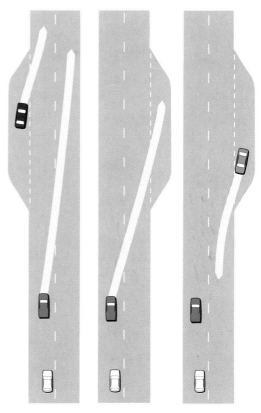

In each of these situations approaching lay-bys, the white car should beware of overtaking. The arrows show the possible actions of traffic ahead.

that there are fast-moving vehicles approaching you on the sections of road you cannot see. Follow the basic rule for overtaking.

Identify a gap into which you can return and the point along the road at which you will be able to enter it.

Judge whether you will be able to reach that point before any approaching vehicle, seen or unseen, could come into conflict with you.

You should have observed the whole stretch of road necessary to complete the manoeuvre, and know that it does not include any other hazards. Look especially for hazards which might cause the vehicles you are overtaking to alter their position. Make full use of road signs and road markings, especially those giving instructions or warning you of hazards ahead.

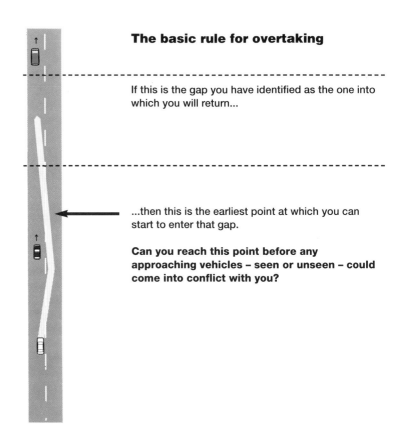

The basic rule for overtaking

If this is the gap you have identified as the one into which you will return...

...then this is the earliest point at which you can start to enter that gap.

Can you reach this point before any approaching vehicles – seen or unseen – could come into conflict with you?

Road surface

The condition of the road surface should always be taken into account before you overtake. There may be ruts or holes which could throw a vehicle off course, or surface water which could cause a curtain of spray at a critical moment. The effects of adverse weather on road holding and visibility must always be taken into account.

See Chapter 3, Observation, page 44.

Overtaking in a stream of vehicles

Overtaking in a stream of vehicles is more difficult because it takes more time. You also have to take into account the possible actions of more drivers both in front and behind. There is always the possibility that drivers in front are not aware of your presence or intention to overtake and that drivers behind might attempt to overtake you.

Before overtaking, you should identify a clear gap between the vehicles in front which you can enter safely. Be aware that the gap may close up before you arrive, so choose gaps that are large enough to allow for this. Do not overtake if you will have to force your vehicle into a gap.

When considering overtaking in a stream of vehicles, it may be an advantage to position your vehicle on the offside section of the road, but be aware of the dangers of this position. Also be aware that following drivers might close up the gap that you have just left, preventing you from returning to it. An offside position can improve your viewpoint because it is not obstructed by the vehicles in front, but this depends on the road layout. You can gain by holding this position if you can see that the road ahead is clear, and if you can identify a clear return gap and have sufficient time in which to reach it. When you reach the first return gap you may not need to enter it. If it is safe, hold the offside position to assess the possibility for further overtaking.

When you overtake clusters of vehicles, you must take extra care to ensure that the other drivers are aware of your presence.

Where a queue has formed because of an obstruction in the road ahead, do not attempt to jump the queue. This invariably annoys other road users and can be dangerous.

Overtaking on a single carriageway

Overtaking on a single carriageway is perhaps the most hazardous form of overtaking. While you are overtaking, your vehicle is in the path of any oncoming vehicles so great care must be taken before deciding on the manoeuvre.

Develop the ability to judge the speed and distance of oncoming vehicles accurately. You need to be able to assess whether you can reach the return gap before they do. Remember you always have the option of deciding not to overtake. Judging the speed of an oncoming vehicle is extremely difficult, especially on long straight roads. The size and type of the approaching vehicle may give you an indication of its possible speed.

Plan and prepare your overtaking carefully. As well as looking for vehicles, train yourself to look specifically for motorcyclists, cyclists and pedestrians before you overtake. If you do not expect to see something, you may not see it when it is there – an oncoming pedestrian or cyclist can be easily overlooked.

Overtaking on bends

Right-hand bends

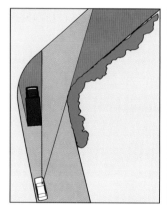 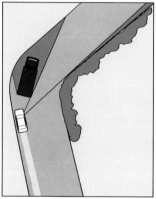 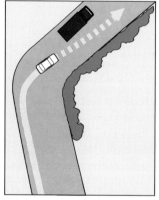

Where the vehicle in front is approaching the apex of a right-hand bend with a restricted view, you should select a course well to the nearside.

Move up on the vehicle in front just before it reaches the apex so that you gain the earliest possible view along its offside.

Overtake if the road is clear, as long as there is no risk of losing tyre adhesion and you have adequate nearside clearance during the manoeuvre. If conditions are not favourable for overtaking, drop back.

obstructed vision

Left-hand bends

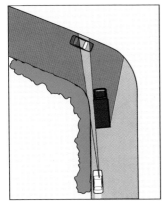

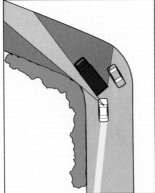

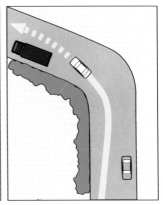

Where the leading vehicle approaches a blind left bend do not attempt to overtake until you have a clear view of the road ahead.

You could maintain a position where you can see along the nearside of the leading vehicle as it passes through the bend.

If this view is favourable move out to look along the offside as the road straightens and start to overtake when conditions are suitable. Bear in mind that areas of the road will be obscured while you change from a nearside to an offside view, so take great care when you do this.

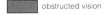 obstructed vision

Single carriageway roads marked with three lanes

Single carriageway roads marked with three lanes are potentially very dangerous as the overtaking lane in each direction is the shared centre lane. Never attempt to overtake on such a road if there is the possibility of an approaching vehicle moving into the centre lane. Avoid overtaking when you would make a third line of moving vehicles unless you are sure it is absolutely safe to do so.

Avoid the temptation to follow another vehicle through an apparently safe gap on a three-lane single carriageway. Always assess a safe return position for yourself. The leading vehicle may well be able to slip safely into place on the nearside leaving you stranded in the middle faced by oncoming vehicles.

When you are judging speed and distance to overtake and a vehicle is approaching, look out for the presence of the 'lurker'. This is a vehicle which closes right up behind other vehicles and then sweeps out into full view. Do not assume that the drivers of light vehicles or cars behind a heavy lorry are content to stay where they are. They could well pull out just when you are overtaking.

Overtaking on dual carriageways

On dual carriageways it can be more difficult to judge the speed of traffic approaching from the rear.

See Chapter 10, Motorway driving and the Highway Code.

Before overtaking watch carefully the vehicles in the nearside lanes. If one of them is closing up on the vehicle in front, the driver may pull out, possibly without signalling or only signalling as the vehicle starts to move out. A good guide is the distance between the wheels of the vehicle and the lane markings. If the gap narrows, the vehicle could be moving out. Overtaking when it would cause three vehicles to be abreast should be avoided if possible, although on many motorways this is difficult. You should always overtake on the right on dual carriageways except when traffic is moving in queues and the queue on the right is moving more slowly than you are.

Practise observation skills for overtaking

Over the next two weeks make a note of any overtaking situations that you misjudge. Add to this list any dangerous or potentially dangerous misjudgements you can remember making in the past. For each situation work out the observational errors that caused you to misjudge the situation.

Ask yourself if any errors occur consistently. Do you make specific errors such as failing to take account of obscured junctions, or is the problem a general lack of observation? Plan how to improve your observation so that you can avoid making the same mistakes in the future.

Assisting others to overtake

Assisting others to overtake eases tensions and improves the quality of driving for everyone on the road. The key element is your attitude of mind when you drive. You should not regard driving as a competition but as a means of travelling between two points as safely as possible. Try to regard your driving dispassionately and keep an eye on yourself to identify any inappropriate responses. If other drivers wish to overtake you, assist them:

- be alert to the intentions of drivers behind you: use your mirrors and assess whether they wish to overtake or not
- allow enough distance between you and the vehicle in front for the overtaking vehicle to enter the gap.

Be aware of the likely dangers on the approach and exit from areas where the speed limit is lower than the national speed limit. Other drivers are quite likely to attempt to overtake you while you observe the legal speed limit. This is likely to happen:

- when you slow down to enter a lower speed limit area
- when you are about to leave a lower speed limit area.

Review

In this chapter we have looked at:

how to overtake safely

how to overtake in the absence of other hazards

the three-stage approach to overtaking when other hazards cause you to take up a following position

the hazards that you should consider before overtaking.

Check your understanding

What makes overtaking potentially hazardous?

What are the seven safety points that you should follow for overtaking?

If you are in doubt about overtaking what should you do?

What are the hazards that would make it necessary to follow another vehicle before overtaking?

What is the three-stage approach to overtaking and when is it used?

When you move out before overtaking, what should you check?

What do you need to consider about the driver in front before overtaking?

What do you need to consider about road layout and conditions before overtaking?

When can it be useful to hold an offside position?

How can you help others to overtake?

If you have difficulty in answering any of these questions, look back over the relevant part of this chapter to refresh your memory.

Chapter 10

Motorway driving

Developing your skill at motorway driving

Safe motorway driving depends on the careful application of the skills and methods of driving that you have learnt in the other chapters of *Roadcraft*, together with an awareness of the extra hazards that arise from the speed and volume of the traffic. This chapter identifies those hazards and ways of dealing with them. You do not need to develop special techniques for dealing with motorways, but you do have to apply the techniques you have learnt all the more rigorously because of the testing conditions.

Although this chapter is called motorway driving much of it is applicable to driving on dual carriageways. The speed limit for cars is the same on many dual carriageways as it is on motorways, but the absence of a hard shoulder and the presence of lay-bys and crossroads make dual carriageways especially hazardous.

Before you join the motorway

The *Highway Code*

The *Highway Code* contains advice on motorway driving, and includes information on motorway signs and regulations. You should know these sections thoroughly. This chapter discusses the techniques which will help you to implement the *Highway Code* advice more effectively.

Special features of motorways

You need to prepare adequately before you join a motorway. These are the special conditions you should consider:

  the speed and volume of the traffic

  the limited occurrence of refreshment and refuelling areas

the dangers of stopping on the hard shoulder

the level of attention required

the legal limitations on certain vehicles using the motorway.

Each of these affects your safety. High speeds mean that hazardous situations develop quickly and that you travel further before you can react. Minimum stopping distances are greatly extended and collisions often cause serious injury and damage. As the volume of traffic increases, the demands on your attention and decision-making also increase. With more vehicles there are more hazards and the opportunities for manoeuvre are more restricted.

You need to maintain a high level of attention, which is difficult in monotonous conditions. Fatigue is a real problem and you should always plan adequate rest-breaks. The limited opportunities for stopping on motorways require drivers to be in good health and their vehicles in good condition. The risk of collision makes stopping on the hard shoulder extremely hazardous for the occupants of the stationary vehicle and for other motorway users.

We shall now look at the safety implications of these special features of motorways for:

the driver

the vehicle

the road conditions.

The driver

The high speeds of motorway traffic cause dangerous situations to develop very rapidly. Experience is required to cope with your own speed and the speed of other vehicles. Accurately assessing high speeds and stopping distances at these speeds takes time to develop. Always drive well within your own competence and aim to steadily develop your experience so that you are fully comfortable within your existing speed range before moving on to higher speeds.

Fatigue

Fatigue causes a disproportionate number of accidents on motorways. As you tire your ability to take in and process information is reduced and your ability to react to the information you have received takes longer. Fatigue is most likely in conditions which are relatively unchanging – for example, driving for long periods in lower density traffic, or in fog or at night. You should know how to cope with fatigue. This is fully discussed in Chapter 1 so look back and refresh your memory if necessary.

See Chapter 1,
Becoming a better
driver, page 16,
Fatigue.

Health, medication and emotional state

You should not drive when you feel unwell. This is particularly important on motorways because of the dangers of high-speed accidents and the limited opportunities to stop if you feel ill. Medication is a common source of drowsiness, so if you are taking medicine follow any advice on the container or given by your doctor about driving. Your emotional state affects your ability to recognise hazards, to take appropriate decisions and to implement them efficiently. If you are emotionally distressed you should be aware of the effect that it is likely to have on your driving.

Time pressure and the purpose of your journey

Police drivers are trained to respond to urgent calls without taking undue risks. It is nevertheless a fact that drivers who feel their journey is urgent, either because of time pressure or because of the purpose of the journey, tend to respond less safely to hazards and take more risks. A sense of urgency does not give the right to take risks. No emergency is so great that it justifies the possibility of injuring or killing someone through bad driving.

Route plan

Plan your route and know where your rest points and point of exit are before you undertake a motorway journey. Consulting maps to identify rest places and points of exit while you are driving is dangerous, and must not be done on motorways or any other road.

The vehicle

Your vehicle should be safe and legal before driving on a motorway or any other road. Remember to carry out a roadworthiness check before you start your journey.

See Roadworthiness
check, page 170.

Before you start a motorway journey, run through a 'POWER' check:

Petrol **O**il **W**ater **E**lectrics **R**ubber *(tyres and wipers)*

Road conditions

Consider the likely traffic volume and the possibility of roadworks and other delays. These affect how long your journey will take, and allowances should be made for them so that you are not rushing to meet deadlines. As delays mount up it may be worth considering another route or cancelling your journey altogether. Where weather conditions are deteriorating you should consider very carefully whether to make your journey at all. In foggy conditions it is essential that you are familiar with the *Highway Code* fog code and use it. Further advice on fog is given below and in Chapter 3. Your safety depends on adapting your driving to the prevailing road and weather conditions and this is especially crucial on motorways.

Joining the motorway

Which lane is which?

This chapter uses the numbering system used by the police and other emergency services to refer to motorway lanes.

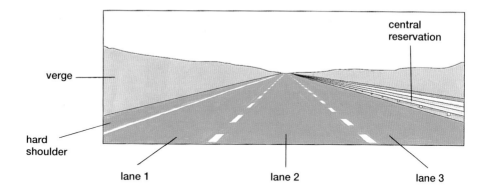

The nearside lane is lane 1, and the other lanes are numbered in sequence to the furthest offside lane. On a three-lane motorway lane 1 is the lane next to the hard shoulder and lane 3 is the lane next to the central reservation. The hard shoulder is not counted as a carriageway lane.

Joining the motorway at a slip road or where motorways merge is hazardous and you should use the system of car control to approach and join. Slip roads are designed to give drivers the time and space to merge smoothly with traffic on the main carriageway. They are often elevated and you should take advantage of the high viewpoint to observe the traffic flow and to plan your approach. Skilful use of the system should enable you to join the motorway without causing other drivers to alter course or speed. Drivers on the motorway have priority and may not be able to move over to allow you to enter, but with early vision, planning and acceleration sense you should be able to merge safely. Only poor planning or exceptionally heavy traffic will cause you to stop in the acceleration lane.

Slip roads have one or more lanes. If you are travelling in an offside lane of the slip road, consider how your speed and position will affect the access of nearside vehicles on to the motorway. If you overtake a vehicle to your nearside just before joining the motorway you could block its path. You are in danger of colliding with it if you cannot move straight into lane 2 of the motorway.

Do not overtake a vehicle travelling in the inside lane of the slip road if this would block the entry of that vehicle on to the motorway.

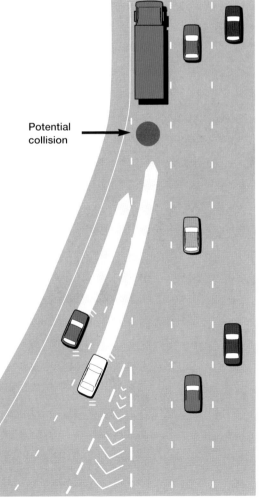

Potential collision

Use the system

As you enter the motorway all five phases of the system are relevant. You need to take sufficient **information** about the traffic on the slip road and motorway to ensure that you are in the right **position**, at the right **speed**, in the right **gear** to **accelerate** on to the motorway smoothly and in safety.

Signalling

As you are about to enter lane 1 of the motorway consider giving a signal to inform motorists already on the motorway of your intention to join the traffic flow.

Before you join the motorway check over your shoulder to make sure there is nothing in your blind spot.

Acceleration

As the speeds on motorways are higher than on the rest of the road system, you should allow yourself time to adjust to driving at speed and to the speeds of other vehicles.

Observation

Because of the speeds involved, extended observation on the motorway is essential:

- look ahead and behind you right up to the road horizons
- scan ahead, to the sides and to the rear frequently and thoroughly
- use your mirrors regularly – you should know at all times what is happening behind you
- be aware of the blind spots on your vehicle and those of other drivers and be prepared to move your body and alter vehicle position to observe what is happening in those areas
- monitor what is happening to your vehicle – regularly check that the instruments are giving normal readings, listen to the sound of your engine and to the noise of the tyres on the road surface
- check your speed regularly on the speedometer – it is very easy to increase speed without realising it.

Adapting to higher speeds

At 70 miles per hour you travel 31 metres per second (over 100 ft per second). At such speeds you need as much time to react as possible:

extend your observations in all directions and to the road horizons to give yourself more time

anticipate early and maintain a safe following distance – in good weather the two-second rule provides a good guide but in poor weather conditions this distance needs to be greatly extended

avoid coarse steering at speed

give other drivers sufficient time to see your signals before making a manoeuvre

wind and engine noise can drown the sound of your horn at high speeds, so consider using your headlights as an effective alternative.

*See Chapter 3,
Observation, page 38,
Scanning
and Chapter 4,
Acceleration, using
gears, braking and
steering, page 67, The
safe stopping distance
rule.*

On your next three motorway journeys, practise extending your observation. Make a point of scanning as far as the road horizon, front and back. Use your mirrors frequently. Regularly scan to the sides as well.

Your aim is to equip yourself with the longest possible time in which to react. Active scanning helps you to maintain a generally high level of attention, which increases your overall safety.

Lane discipline

Good lane discipline is essential for motorway driving. There are no slow or fast lanes. Overtake only to the right, except when traffic is moving in queues and the queue on your right is moving more slowly than you are.

Do not move to a lane on your left to overtake.

Overtaking

Before overtaking be alert for:

slower vehicles moving out in front of you

faster vehicles coming up behind you.

Apply the system of car control to overtake safely on motorways and pay special attention to the information phase.

Taking information

The high speeds of motorway traffic make it necessary to take information carefully before making any manoeuvre. Scan regularly so that you are continually aware of the pattern of surrounding traffic. You should know which vehicles are closing up on other vehicles in front, and which vehicles are moving up behind. Constantly monitor opportunities to overtake and match your speed of approach to coincide with an opportunity. Make allowances for the additional hazards presented by lane closures and motorway junctions.

Look for early warnings of the intention of other drivers to overtake. Indications of another driver's intention to move out are:

- relative speeds
- head movements
- body movements
- vehicle movement from the centre of the lane towards the white lane markers.

You are likely to see all these before the driver signals: many drivers only signal as they start to change lanes.

Over a motorway journey of reasonable length (say 20 miles), practise watching for the indications above and try to predict, before they start indicating, when other drivers are about to change lanes.

Use this anticipation to help your planning.

Overtaking on left-hand bends when lanes 1 and 2 are mainly occupied by heavy goods or large vehicles needs to be considered carefully. There is always the possibility that a car is hidden between the heavy goods vehicles and is about to pull out into lane 3. In these circumstances make sure you can stop in the distance you can see to be clear. Do not attempt to overtake unless you are sure you can see all the vehicles in lane 2 and well into the gaps between them so you can be sure no small vehicles are concealed.

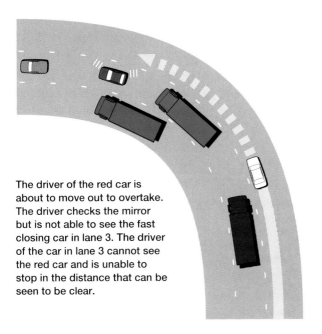

The driver of the red car is about to move out to overtake. The driver checks the mirror but is not able to see the fast closing car in lane 3. The driver of the car in lane 3 cannot see the red car and is unable to stop in the distance that can be seen to be clear.

As you move from lane 1 to lane 2, beware of vehicles moving up behind you into lane 2 from lane 3.

Just before you overtake make a thorough check of the position and speed of the vehicles behind. Move your head to reduce the extent of the blind spot. Re-check the position and speed of vehicles to the front and then consider the information that you need to give to the surrounding traffic.

Giving information

Consider alerting other drivers to your presence especially if you are travelling at speed. If you decide a headlight signal would be helpful, give it in sufficient time for the other driver to react. The purpose of a headlight warning is to inform other drivers of your presence. Give a single flash, extending its length according to your speed and the response of other drivers. Take care not to appear aggressive to other drivers, and be aware of the possibility of dazzling oncoming drivers. Also be careful that your headlight flash is not misinterpreted as an invitation to other drivers to move out in front of you.

Indicator signals

Consider giving an indicator signal before changing lanes. Let the indicator flash long enough for other drivers to see and react to it.

When you have passed the vehicle or vehicles in front, return to the appropriate lane when a suitable opportunity arises but avoid excessive weaving.

Overtaking situations to avoid

You should generally avoid overtaking when to do so would create a line of three vehicles travelling abreast. In current traffic conditions this is often not possible but you should avoid situations like the one illustrated below which leave you no room for manoeuvre.

This illustrates a problem for vehicles moving at speed and overtaking three abreast. The overtaking driver in the white car has no room for manoeuvre if a hazard arises. Movement into lane 1 or 2 is blocked by the vehicles in those lanes and escape through lane 3 is blocked by the vehicle ahead. Hold back until the vehicle in lane 3 has moved ahead of the vehicles in lane 2. This then gives you the option of an alternative position. Keep a watchful eye on your mirrors for vehicles closing up fast behind you.

Being overtaken

Anticipate the movement of vehicles behind you by their lane position and their speed of approach. By observing minor details in the way the traffic is behaving you will be forewarned before any signals or manoeuvres are made. This will help you to avoid potentially dangerous situations. Be aware that, as you are overtaken, you temporarily enter a blind spot for the overtaking driver.

Motorway junctions

At junctions and service areas, there are likely to be variations in the speed of the traffic flow and an increase in the number of vehicles changing lanes. Watch for drivers who delay changing lanes for an exit to the last second. When you see a motorway exit, anticipate the possibility of an entry slip road ahead and traffic joining the motorway.

If you are on the main carriageway, check your mirrors early and if possible allow traffic to join the motorway by making slight adjustments to your speed or changing to a lane on your right. However, do not move to a lane on your right if it forces existing motorway users to change their speed or position. Ultimately it is the vehicle joining the motorway that should give way.

Watch for drivers who delay changing lanes for an exit road to the last second, and watch for traffic joining the motorway by slip roads ahead.

Leaving the motorway

Leaving the motorway should be carefully planned. Know well in advance at which junction you intend to leave. Assess the road and traffic conditions as you approach it and make use of the information provided by road signs and markings.

Exit information

The diagram below illustrates the exit information given at most motorway exits.

One mile from the exit a direction sign gives the junction number and the roads leading off the exit	At a half mile from the exit the same information is repeated on the direction sign plus the town or destination names	At 300 yards from the exit deceleration lane there is a marker post	Further marker posts are positioned at the 200 yard and 100 yard point before the start of the deceleration lane	A third large sign at the beginning of the deceleration lane also adds principal destinations ahead

As you approach your intended exit junction look for the advance direction boards and use the system of car control to plan and carry out your exit. If the motorway is busy, consider joining the left-hand lane earlier rather than later. Always allow sufficient time for other drivers to react to your signals. Generally you should indicate no later than the 300 yard marker and if it would benefit other drivers you should indicate well before.

Avoid braking on the main carriageway if possible and plan to lose any unwanted road speed in the deceleration lane. On busy motorways be alert for vehicles attempting to leave the motorway late from the second or third lane and cutting across your path. Remember that high speeds will affect your perception of speed when you leave the motorway:

- check your speedometer regularly to help you adjust to the slower speeds of the ordinary road system
- plan for the point at which you will meet two-way traffic
- be alert for acute bends at the end of exit slip roads and watch for oil and tyre dust deposits which make these areas exceptionally slippery.

Over the next month pay attention to the way you use the system of car control to leave a motorway. Include starting your exit from a position in lanes 1, 2 and 3. Pay particular attention to the information phase. After you have completed an exit assess whether it went according to your driving plan, and whether you considered all the relevant phases of the system. If not, work out how you could improve the manoeuvre next time.

A route direction sign is usually placed at the point where the deceleration lane separates from the main carriageway

Special hazards

There are a number of special hazards which you need to take account of on motorway journeys. At high speeds overall safe stopping distances greatly increase. Safe driving depends on the basic rule: always drive so that you are able to stop in the distance you can see to be clear. This will vary with the density of traffic, weather conditions and the other hazards described in this section. If this advice were systematically followed motorway pile-ups would not occur.

Weather conditions

For further advice about dealing with the weather conditions described in this section, see Chapter 3, Observation, pages 42–44, Weather conditions.

Poor weather conditions can reduce visibility and road holding. At high speed the effects of these hazards are increased. When visibility is restricted you must reduce speed and consider using headlights and foglights. You must use them if visibility drops below 100 metres. A useful guide for assessing visibility is the gap between motorway marker posts which is approximately 100 metres. Bear in mind that foglights can mask the brakelights and dazzle the driver behind and you must switch them off when visibility improves.

Fog

See also the fog code in the Highway Code.

Fog is particularly dangerous on motorways. It reduces drivers' perception of speed and their perception of risk because they cannot see; at the same time it encourages them to drive closer together in order to keep sight of the vehicle lights ahead. Be alert to the risks from the reckless behaviour of other drivers.

In freezing fog, mist and spray rapidly freezes on to the windscreen at higher speeds and further reduces visibility. To stop in the distance you can see to be clear in variable fog you must adjust your speed to the actual density of the fog banks you are driving through, not to some imagined 'safe' speed for foggy conditions. Driving in fog is extremely tiring, so watch for signs of fatigue and take more rest if necessary.

Rain

See Chapter 5, Skidding, page 90, Aquaplaning, for further advice.

At speed the hazards from rain and water lying on the surface of the road increase. Heavy spray caused by tyres cutting through water can reduce visibility to a few feet, and you should allow for this, especially while overtaking. Water lying on the road surface can build up to form a wedge of water between the tyres and the road causing aquaplaning; this results in instantaneous and complete loss of control.

After a long, hot, dry spell a deposit of tyre and other dust builds up on the road surface. These deposits create a slippery surface especially during and after rain. Take precautions to retain tyre grip in these conditions.

Snow and sleet

Snow and sleet reduce visibility and reduce tyre traction. At speed spray thrown up by the wheels of the vehicle in front reduces visibility further, and steering problems arise when ruts develop in the snow. In heavy snow consider whether your journey is really necessary.

Ice

Pay particular attention to your speed and following distances in icy conditions, especially if the freezing conditions have developed suddenly and the road surface is not gritted.

High winds

Motorways are often elevated above the surrounding countryside and tend to suffer from the effects of high winds. Be prepared for particularly strong gusts of wind on leaving cuttings, entering or emerging from under a bridge, crossing dales and going into open country. Take particular care on top of viaducts and bridges.

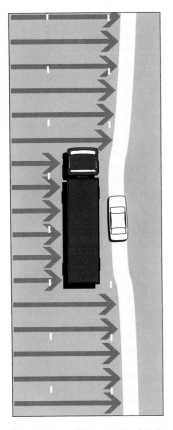

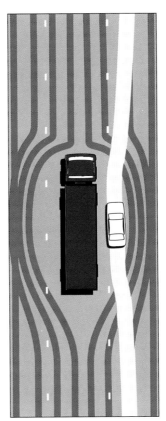

In windy conditions high-sided vehicles may suddenly veer; they also tend to act as wind breaks causing heavy buffeting to smaller vehicles as they draw past them. Keep a firm, two-handed grip on the steering wheel in these conditions.

Wind effects are also caused by the slip stream of high-sided vehicles. This pulls smaller vehicles towards the larger vehicle during overtaking. As the smaller vehicle moves in front it breaks free of the suction and has a tendency to veer away. Counter this by a firm grip and appropriate pressure on the steering wheel.

Bright sun

Bright sunshine in the hours just after sunrise and before sunset can cause serious dazzle, especially on east/west sections of road; consider using your visors. When the sun is shining in your mirrors, adjust them to give you the best visibility with the minimum of glare. Be aware that drivers in front will have similar problems in seeing behind, and allow for this when overtaking.

Debris

Regularly scan the road surface for debris which may have fallen from vehicles. This can cause other vehicles to suddenly alter course and can damage tyres.

Lane closures

Roadworks are regularly encountered on motorway journeys. Contraflow systems are not dangerous in themselves but become dangerous when drivers fail to respond to advance warnings. All roadworks are signed on approach and the sequence of the signs is always the same and should be known. You should conform to the mandatory speed limits that often accompany roadworks, even when conditions seem to be suitable for a higher speed.

Merging with other traffic requires judgement and courtesy. A sensible policy is for vehicles from each lane to merge alternately. These situations have great potential for unnecessary conflict and therefore unnecessary accidents. Allow adequate following gaps, and do not close up tightly to prevent other vehicles merging. Drivers in the closed lane should avoid causing provocation by overtaking long queues of traffic waiting in the open lanes.

Matrix signs warn of hazards that may be some distance ahead.

Matrix signs and signals are used on motorways to warn of lane closures or other changes in driving conditions ahead. You may not immediately be able to see the need to slow down or change lanes. Do not be complacent and assume the sign is a mistake. The incident it refers to may be some distance along the motorway.

General safety rules

Although there are fewer accidents per mile travelled on motorways than other roads, they can be extremely hazardous places. You should follow these general safety rules at all times:

- maintain lane discipline at all times

- maintain a safe following distance at all times – avoid driving too close to the vehicle in front

- always be able to stop safely in the distance you can see to be clear

- do not walk on the carriageway

- do not reverse along the carriageway

- do not turn to look at accidents on your own or the other carriageway but anticipate the likelihood of other drivers slowing down to look

- do not use or block emergency crossing points

- plan your route in advance – know your intended exit junction number

- be alert and take active steps to prevent boredom and fatigue

- concentrate fully and use your mirrors often

- give signals in plenty of time

- know the meanings of the different road signs, matrix and gantry signals used on motorways.

Review

In this chapter we have looked at:

the special features of motorways

why motorways can be hazardous

what safety points you should always consider about the driver, the vehicle and road conditions before you use a motorway

how to identify the lanes of a motorway

how to join a motorway

the importance of extended observation, especially when driving at speed

how to overtake on a motorway

the additional hazards at motorway junctions

how to leave a motorway

weather conditions and other special hazards to consider

what to do at lane closures

general safety rules for driving on motorways.

Check your understanding

What are the special features of motorways that you need to consider before starting a journey?

Why should you not drive on a motorway if you are feeling tired or unwell?

Why can it be hazardous to overtake a vehicle on the acceleration lane just as you join a motorway?

At 70 mph how many metres do you travel in one second?

Apart from indicator lights, what are the possible early signs that another vehicle is going to change lanes?

What signals might you consider giving before overtaking?

What is the typical series of signs, starting from the 1 mile sign, that mark a motorway exit junction?

What lights should you have on when visibility is below 100 metres on the motorway?

What speed should you drive at in fog?

Describe at least three other hazards that can create particular problems on motorways, and explain how you would plan to deal with them.

If you have difficulty in answering any of these questions, look back over the relevant part of this chapter to refresh your memory.

Speed and safety

Safety

The first part of this chapter looks at the effects of speed on safety and at the factors you must consider when assessing a safe speed: these include the capabilities of the driver and the vehicle, and the prevailing road traffic and weather conditions. The second part of the chapter looks in detail at how speed affects the driver and at the key points that will help you to use speed safely.

Speed has a major impact on safety. International evidence clearly shows that lower speed limits result in fewer accidents. In Chapter 1 we saw that drivers who drive fast regardless of the circumstances have an accident risk three to five times greater than drivers who do not. At greater speeds the risks obviously increase – you approach hazards faster, you have less time to react, and the impact damage is greater. A child hit by a car at 20 mph may be injured but will probably live; a child hit at 40 mph will probably die.

There is an inherent risk in speed but whatever your speed, if it is inappropriate in the circumstances, it is dangerous. This concept is central to the system of car control and you will have encountered the idea throughout *Roadcraft*. It is most clearly expressed in the safe stopping distance rule:

Drive so that you are able to stop safely on your own side of the road in the distance you can see to be clear.

This rule identifies the maximum speed at which it is safe to drive. It requires you to take account of all the circumstances before deciding the appropriate speed and to adjust your speed as circumstances alter. The capabilities of the driver and vehicle, and the prevailing road, traffic and weather conditions must all be taken into account.

The driver

As we saw in Chapter 1 there are both internal and external pressures which will at times encourage you to drive faster than your competence or the circumstances justify. Skilful drivers

Always drive within your competence, at a speed which is appropriate to the circumstances.

recognise these pressures and take steps to counter them. As you become more experienced your level of confidence may increase but this will not necessarily make you a safer driver. You will only be safe if you also develop appropriate attitudes,

Do you always drive within your competence? Can you recall situations when you were driving too fast for your own comfort? If so, why was it? Were any of the situations similar? How can you avoid repeating them in the future?

The vehicle

Different vehicles have different handling characteristics. When you drive an unfamiliar vehicle allow yourself time to get used to its controls and handling characteristics before driving fast. Allow an extra safety margin until you are confident about how the vehicle will respond.

Road, weather and traffic conditions

When you adapt your speed to the prevailing circumstances you must anticipate and plan for potential as well as actual dangers. This principle underlies all aspects of *Roadcraft* and is extensively covered in earlier chapters.

Speed limits

Statutory maximum speed limits are not the same thing as the *safe* speed.

Statutory speed limits set the maximum permissible speed, but this is not the same thing as a safe speed. The safe speed for a particular stretch of road is determined by the conditions at the time. In winter, at night, in conditions of low visibility or high traffic volume the statutory speed limit may well be excessive. The onus is always on the driver to select a speed appropriate for the conditions.

How speed affects the driver

Vision

As you drive faster, the nearest point at which you can accurately focus moves away from you. Foreground detail becomes blurred and observation becomes more difficult because you have to process more information in less time. The only way to cope with this is to scan further ahead, so that you gain more time to assess, plan and react. In complicated situations or where there is a lot of foreground information – in a busy shopping street, for example – you need to go more slowly to observe and process the information adequately.

See Chapter 3, Observation, page 39, How speed affects observation, for more information.

Underestimating speed

It is easy to underestimate the speed at which you are driving. Speed perception is complicated and depends on several factors such as:

- the difference in detail perceived by your forward and side vision
- the engine, road and wind noise
- the unevenness of the ride
- what you regard as a normal speed
- how wide the road is and whether it is enclosed or open
- your height off the ground.

Alterations to any of these factors can alter your perception of speed. The list that follows gives some common situations where speed perception can be distorted. The solution is simple – keep a check on your speedometer.

When you have been travelling at high speed on a motorway or other fast road and then transfer to roads where speeds below 30 or 40 mph are appropriate, these slower speeds will seem much slower than they really are. Allow time for normal speed perception to return.

When visibility is low – in fog, sleet, heavy rain and at night – speed perceptions become distorted and it is easy to drive faster than you realise.

When driving a vehicle that is smoother, quieter or more powerful than your usual vehicle, it is easy to drive too fast. As well as sight and balance, you use other senses to assess speed: road noise, engine noise and vibration all play a part.

When one or more of these is reduced, it can seem that you are going slower than you really are.

- On wide open roads, speeds will seem slower than on small confined roads.

Check your speedometer whenever you leave a motorway or high speed road, especially at roundabouts.

Check your safety at speed

Over a journey of about one and a half hours, monitor whether you always drive so that you are able to stop on your own side of the road in the distance you can see to be clear.

Do you really know in practice what distance it will take you to stop at 20, 30, 40 and 50 mph? (See page 68.)

Is there anywhere you can practise stopping from 70 mph in total safety?

If you do not keep to the safe stopping distance rule at higher speeds, why is this so?

Speed and fatigue

See Chapter 1, Becoming a better driver, page 16, Fatigue.

Driving at high speed requires a high level of attention and judgement which you cannot sustain if you are tired. Over long distances this level of concentration is itself fatiguing and you should plan adequate rest periods to recover alertness.

Whatever the pressures to drive faster you must always drive within your own capabilities.

Using speed safely

The skill of driving safely at speed is not easily acquired. Every driver has their own speed limit: this is the highest speed at which they are safe and comfortable in any given situation. You should know what yours is and never go beyond it. At 30 mph a minor driving error may be corrected but at 70 mph the same error could be disastrous.

Speed must always be related to the amount of road you can see to be clear, and the ability to stop within this distance, by day or night. In this respect local knowledge, if wrongly used, can be hazardous because it can tempt you to drive faster than is safe along familiar roads.

You should know the braking characteristics of your vehicle and the table of stopping distances and be able to relate these to the road you are travelling on. Bear in mind that when speed is doubled braking distance quadruples, and that in wet and slippery conditions braking distances increase greatly.

See Chapter 4, Acceleration, using gears, braking and steering, page 68, Braking distance.

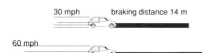

30 mph   braking distance 14 m

60 mph   braking distance 55 m

When speed is doubled, braking distance quadruples.

Overtaking

Driving at high speeds may entail frequent overtaking. Overtaking at speed demands careful preparation, positioning, observation and judgement of speed and distance. It is safest when carried out using the system of car control combined with a full awareness of possible hazards.

See Chapter 9, Overtaking.

Driving safely at speed depends above all else on adapting your speed to the circumstances. The faster you go the less time you have to react and the more disastrous the possible consequences.

Key safety points

These are the key points to remember:

- do not drive at speed unless you are competent, and it is safe to do so

- be familiar with the controls and the handling characteristics of your vehicle – use the controls smoothly

- high-speed driving requires maximum attentiveness – if you cannot achieve a high level of attentiveness because of fatigue or some other cause, do not drive

- always drive so that you can stop within the distance you can see to be clear, by day or by night

- if you double your speed you quadruple your braking distance

- put into practice the skills developed in *Roadcraft* which are designed to maximise safety

- be aware of the onset of fatigue, and take appropriate action

- no emergency is so great that it justifies an accident – it is far better to arrive late than not at all.

Review

In this chapter we have looked at:

why speed affects safety

how to assess a safe speed

the factors which need to be considered when choosing the appropriate speed for the circumstances

how speed affects the driver

situations where it is difficult to assess speed correctly

key points to help you drive safely at speed.

Check your understanding

Why do risks increase as you drive faster?

When is speed dangerous?

What is the safe braking distance rule?

When does urgency justify taking risks?

Is it safe to drive at 30 mph in a built-up area?

Why do you need to drive more slowly in a busy shopping street?

Describe four situations where it can be difficult to accurately assess speed.

If you double your speed, by how much does your braking distance increase?

If you have difficulty in answering any of these questions, look back over the relevant part of this chapter to refresh your memory.

Appendices

Roadworthiness check

Before you start to drive you should ensure that your vehicle is roadworthy. Carry out the following checks:

- [ ] visual examination of the exterior for damage or defects

- [ ] tools and jack are present and in good order

- [ ] wheels in good order and nuts secure
(do not over-tighten, especially with alloy wheels)

- [ ] tyres – check all the tyres, including the spare for:

    - damage

    - tread depth

    - pressure (pressure settings are only accurate when
        tyres are cold)

    - compatibility of type

- [ ] adequate fuel, oil, water, windscreen wash and
other fluids

- [ ] fan belt in good condition and correctly tensioned

- [ ] lights – including high intensity foglights, indicators,
reversing and brakelights – in working order

- [ ] windscreen wipers and washers in good condition

- [ ] horn working correctly

- [ ] fire extinguisher present and in working order

- [ ] all glass clean – windows inside and out, lenses, mirrors.

A useful aid to remember the key points to check is:

P	**O**	**W**	**E**	**R**
petrol	oil	water	electrics	rubber (tyres and wipers)

Pre-driving check

Carry out this check every time you get into a vehicle. Make sure you are familiar with the position and operation of the controls, auxiliary controls and instruments before setting off:

- [ ] handbrake on, gear in neutral

- [ ] identify engine type; type of drive (front, rear or four wheel); type of gearbox (automatic or manual)

- [ ] identify additional driving aids (ABS, traction control, adaptive suspension)

- [ ] adjust seat (position, rake and height if adjustable) to give good all round vision and good access to the controls

- [ ] handbrake and footbrake respond firmly

- [ ] number and position of gears, position of reverse gear

- [ ] position of controls and auxiliaries

- [ ] doors are securely closed.

Switch on ignition, note warning lights; set manual choke if necessary and start engine. Continue with these checks:

- [ ] after system becomes operational check the instruments; if any of the earlier checks could not be completed before ignition or start up, do them now

- [ ] carry out stationary brake test to ensure the system is working

- [ ] adjust mirrors, inside and out, to give best view

- [ ] make sure all the auxiliaries are working

- [ ] check gauges and warning lights

- [ ] check seat belt – not frayed or twisted, locks when tugged, releases on depressing the button, properly adjusted – and then fit it

- [ ] check in mirrors, select gear, check over shoulder, release handbrake (in automatics keep footbrake depressed before engaging DRIVE), move off when safe.

As soon as possible after moving off carry out a moving brake test (see page 66). Check the gauges and warning lights at intervals during the journey, take action if necessary.

Glossary

ABS
See *Antilock braking system*

Acceleration sense
The ability to vary vehicle speed in response to changing road and traffic conditions by accurate use of the accelerator. *See page 58*

Antilock braking system
A braking system which retains the ability to steer during harsh or emergency braking. Also known as ABS. *See page 80*

Aquaplaning
A serious loss of steering and braking control caused by a wedge of water building up between the front tyres and the road surface. *See page 90*

Auxiliaries
The auxiliary controls on a vehicle as distinct from the major controls. Examples of the auxiliaries are: horn, indicators, lights, wipers, washers, heater and ventilation controls. *See Controls, Instruments*

Blind spots
Areas around a vehicle which the driver cannot see because the bodywork blocks sight or the mirrors do not cover these areas. *See page 41*

Bottom gear
See *Gears*

Cadence or rhythm braking
A method of braking in slippery conditions which uses repeated application of the brakes to obtain some steering control while braking. The brakes are sharply applied, to momentarily hold

the wheels locked, and then released again to regain steering. This sequence is repeated deliberately until sufficient road speed is lost. Braking occurs while the brakes are on, steering while they are off. *See pages 71, 90*

Camber
The convex slope across a road surface designed to assist drainage. Camber falls from the crown of the road to the edges. It has an effect on cornering which differs according to whether the bend is to the right or the left. *See page 113*

Central differential
The differential in a four wheel drive vehicle which allows the front and rear wheels to revolve at different speeds.

Controls
The major controls of a vehicle are the accelerator, brakes, clutch, gear-stick, steering wheel. *See Auxiliaries, Instruments*

Cornering
Cornering is used to mean driving a car round a corner, curve or bend. Its meaning is not restricted to corners. *See page 109*

Cylinder compression
See *Engine compression*

Engine compression
The compression of gases in the cylinders of an internal combustion engine. Compression uses energy so, when deceleration reduces the fuel supply to the engine, energy for compression is taken from the road wheels, thereby slowing them down.

Engine torque
The turning power developed by an engine.

Following position
The distance at which it is safe to follow a vehicle in front. This distance varies according to the circumstances. *See pages 104, 129*

Gears
The mechanism which converts the engine output into different speed and power combinations at the road wheels. A high gear is a gear which drives the road wheels faster; a low gear is a gear which drives the road wheels more slowly. Top gear is the highest gear; bottom gear is the lowest gear. In most cars top gear is gear 4 or 5; bottom gear is gear 1.

Hazard/hazardous
Any thing or situation that has the potential for danger. *See page 22*

High gear
See Gears

Information phase
First phase of the system of car control which underlies the other phases. *See page 24*

Instruments
The gauges, dials, warning lights, etc of a vehicle that give information about how it is functioning: for example, the speedometer, oil warning light and main beam indicator.
See Auxiliaries, Controls

Limit point
The limit point is the furthest point along a road to which you have an uninterrupted view of the road surface. On a level stretch of road this will be where the right-hand side of the road appears to intersect with the left-hand side of the road. The limit point is used in a system of cornering called limit point analysis.
See page 115

Low gear
See Gears

Nearside
The left side of a vehicle or animal looking forward from the driver's position. *See Offside*

Offside
The right side of a vehicle or animal looking forward from the driver's position. *See Nearside*

Oversteer
The tendency of a vehicle to turn more than you would expect for the amount of turn given to the steering wheel. Contrast with understeer.
See page 112

Overtaking position
The position adopted behind another vehicle in readiness to overtake when a safe opportunity arises. It is closer than the following position and reduces the time you have to react to actions of the vehicle in front. It should only be adopted if you know there are no hazards ahead which might cause the vehicle in front to brake suddenly. *See page 131*

POWER check
An aid for remembering the key items to check before starting a journey:
Petrol **O**il **W**ater **E**lectrics **R**ubber (tyres and wipers). *See page 170*

Pull–push steering
A steering technique. *See page 74*

Red mist
A mental and physiological state which drivers experience when they are so determined to achieve some non-driving objective, such as pursuing a vehicle in front, that they are no longer capable of assessing driving risks realistically. It is associated with a greatly increased accident risk. *See page 7*

Revs
The number of engine revolutions per minute.

Rhythm braking
See Cadence braking

Road users
Any user of the highway: vehicles, cyclists, pedestrians, animals. The term is used to emphasise the need to be aware of everything on the highway, not just vehicles.

Roadside marker posts
Posts marking the edge of the road, displaying red reflective studs on the nearside of the road

and white reflective studs on the offside of the road.

Rotational steering

A steering technique. *See page 75*

Safe stopping distance rule

This rule is one of the basic safety considerations when driving. It controls your speed by relating speed to the ability to stop. Always drive so that you are able to stop on your own side of the road in the distance you can see to be clear. *See page 67*

Scanning

Method of observation. The use of regular visual sweeps of the whole of the driving environment – the distance, the mid-ground, the foreground, sides and rear – to ensure that the driver is aware of everything that is happening.
See pages 15, 38

Superelevation

Superelevation is the banking up of a section of road towards the outside edge of the curve. This makes the slope favourable for cornering in both directions. *See page 113*

The system – the system of car control

A systematic way of approaching and negotiating hazards that emphasises safety and is central to *Roadcraft*. It is fully explained in Chapter 2.

Top gear

See Gears

Traction

The grip of a tyre on the road surface.

Traction control systems

Traction control improves vehicle stability and assists steering by controlling excess wheel slip on individual wheels and reducing engine power to maintain tyre grip. *See page 80*

Tyre grip trade-off

The tyre grip available in any given situation is limited, and is shared between accelerating, braking and steering forces. If more of the tyre grip is used for braking or accelerating, less will be available for steering.
See pages 55, 110

Understeer

The tendency of a vehicle to turn less than you expect for the amount of turn you give to the steering wheel. Contrast with oversteer.
See page 112

Undertaking

Overtaking on the nearside in situations which contravene the *Highway Code*.

Wheel slip

The difference between the velocity of the vehicle and the velocity of the outer circumference of the tyre, usually expressed as a percentage.

Index